THREE AMERICAN ORIGINALS

THREE AMERICAN

ORIGINALS

by Joseph W. Reed

 WESLEYAN UNIVERSITY PRESS
Middletown, Connecticut

JOHN FORD,

WILLIAM FAULKNER, &

CHARLES IVES

Also by Joseph W. Reed

English Biography in the Early Nineteenth Century (1800–1838)
Faulkner's Narrative

EDITOR

Barbara Bodichon's American Diary, 1857–1858
The Business of Motion Pictures
With G. R. Creeger, *Selected Prose and Poetry of the Romantic Era*
With Wilmarth S. Lewis, *Walpole's Castle of Otranto*
With Jeanine Basinger and John Frazer, *Working with Kazan*
With W. S. Lewis, *Walpole's Family Correspondence*. The Yale
    Edition of Horace Walpole's Correspondence, Vol. 36
With Frederick A. Pottle, *Boswell, Laird of Auchinleck*. The Yale
    Edition of the Private Papers of James Boswell, Vol. XI

GENERAL EDITOR

Sesquicentennial Papers, Wesleyan University

All inquiries and permissions requests should be addressed to the
Publisher, Wesleyan University Press, 110 Mt. Vernon Street,
Middletown, Connecticut 06457.

Distributed by Harper & Row Publishers, Keystone Industrial Park,
Scranton, Pennsylvania 18512.

LIBRARY OF CONGRESS CATALOGING IN PUBLICATION DATA
Reed, Joseph W., 1932–
    Three American originals.
    Bibliography: p. 173ff.
    1. Arts, Modern—20th century—United States.   2. Faulkner,
William, 1897–1962.   3. Ford, John, 1895–1973.   4. Ives, Charles,
1874–1954.
I. Title.
NX504.R4   1984   700'.92'2   83-23349
ISBN 0-8195-5101-5. (alk. paper)

Manufactured in the United States of America

FIRST EDITION

To Tom Whedon

For what it's worth
Ours is the earth
We'll be a man, my son!

It stands something like this: That an interest in any art-activity, from poetry to baseball is better, broadly speaking, if held as a part of life, or of a life, than if it sets itself up as a whole,—a condition verging, perhaps, toward a monopoly or possibly a kind of atrophy of the other important values, and hence reacting unfavorably upon itself. In the former condition, this interest, this instinctive impulse, this desire to pass from "minor to major," this artistic-intuition or whatever you call it, may have a better chance to be more natural, more comprehensive, perhaps, freer and so more tolerant,—it may develop more muscle in the hind legs and so find a broader vantage ground for jumping to the top of a fence, and more interest in looking around,—if it happens to get there.

—CHARLES IVES, *114 Songs*, Postface

The American we know—the American which we and foreigners so often laugh at and despise—the American in ourselves who is often the subject of our own despair—the joiner, the go-getter, the moralizer; the businessman with ulcers; the clubwoman who cannot remember one word of the morning lecture; the millions in the movie houses gazing at soothing lies—all, all . . . are very busy doing something of great importance. They don't know it and they often do it awkwardly and fall short. They are inventing a new kind of human being—a new relationship between one human being and another—a new relationship between the individual and the all. It is very occupying; it takes an immense toll in shattered lives and minds. It is not easy to be an American because the rules aren't made yet; the examplars are not clear. It is like leaving the Known and Comforting and crossing an ocean into a trackless wilderness in which one must decide what should be taught in the schools and one must build a church. And one can't rely very much on those one knew before—over there, because, for us, those weren't quite right.

—THORNTON WILDER, *The Norton Lectures*

PREFACE AND ACKNOWLEDGMENTS

I started this study of William Faulkner the novelist, John Ford the film director, and Charles Ives the composer with little more than a suspicion that Faulkner, Ford, and Ives have a good deal in common, that the work of any one of them strikes responsive chords in that of either of the other two. It would overstate matters to say that the three are similar artists who simply chose different roads. That difference in road, though, is profound: the art chosen determines much more than the nature of the audience (special or popular) the work will find or the instrumentality of presentation: the choice *determines* the work in every way. It is the three roads chosen that make similarities between the artists difficult to grasp and demonstrate. I have at one time or another posed the problem baldly (in the manner of a game from the past, "Wagner is the Puccini of Music"): what would Ives write for a novel, Ford for a sonata, how would Faulkner direct a film? No answers came, because the question was asked of smart people who realized that it was a question to ponder only: the answer lies beyond an impossibility of such imagining, in the inconceivable zero summer of unrealized works of art. As Faulkner can be only fiction, so Ford can only be film, Ives only music. But the question is useful.

That the answer is inconceivable suggests that the similarities I can assert—similarities artist to artist, or common resemblances across the board—might be of importance and would certainly address a central problem of American Studies—what does America do to its artists? what does being American mean to an artist? The American-ness of these artists and other such heterodox grounds for comparison make this a useful place to try out some modes—comparative biography and cultural context—which have been thought to lie beyond formal critical observation. Once these are admitted to the discussion, the similarities between what we experience in Ford, in Faulkner, and in Ives are striking. And it's another way to avoid the pitfalls of the separateness of the three roads they chose. Heterodoxy and maybe even eccentricity make this study possible. That's one of the gifts of interdisciplinary study.

But the interdisciplinary is tricky. Those who have seen Ford and read Faulkner and heard Ives are quite a narrow enough audience for comparative study without further narrowing the group by requiring readers to have mastered the lingo of film study, the cant of lit. crit., and the obfuscation of music analysis. And I couldn't manage the writing of it. The fully "professional" study of these three artists would be so couched in technicalities and so abuzz with cant words that its usefulness and its interest might be at an end soon after it began.

To be interdisciplinary means more than to announce one's intention to do it: just to be willing to try it doesn't insure that the several disciplines, their measuring sticks, and critical methods will mesh. Clever academics know just to announce that they are interdisciplinary and to ignore the responsibility it implies: part of the responsibility is that translation is necessary, and translation disturbs contented disciplinary habit.

American Studies is marvelously receptive to this kind of translation and reciprocal intellectual exchange. American Studies' failure is that most anybody can gain minimal familiarity with the games, devices, tricks, and gimmicks that go with it; its triumph is that it knows a study under its rubric will never be ideal because a critic within any one of its component disciplines will be disappointed in about two-thirds of what goes on in it.

Translation would be a great deal simpler if Faulkner, Ford, and Ives had come along earlier in the nation's history. Their complex arts are in sophisticated and advanced states, so that the discussion of any individual work of art or single artist's

decision becomes frustratingly specialist. One recourse of sim-
plification is to try to find words that fit all three arts: for composer, novelist, director, read artist; for film, novel, sonata,
read work: for doing what these artists do, read what? But
even this is simple compared to what happens to a word such
as *canon* or *motif*. Every step more along the road to critical
precision leads farther and farther into the technical and farther and farther away from the plain of the general.

I have translated as best I could and have fought lingo and
cant and the temptation to debate. When I taught an under-
graduate course on these artists with Jon Barlow, a Wesleyan
colleague in Music, we took a blunt approach: each tried to
adapt his own critical and analytic tools and shapes so we
could converse. We usually succeeded and found the conversation valuable; neither felt his specialist competence com-
promised. I attempted something like this informal exchange
in writing this book. The audience I address (since I cannot
know what audience I will find) has heard Ives, seen Ford,
read Faulkner, and liked some of what it has seen, read, heard.
Plain language is the aim, jargon the enemy.

I have explored the works of Ford, Faulkner, and Ives here
in three kinds: total *opera*, complete individual work, isolated
passage. But comparison is not a board game: I do not at every
juncture lay out an Ives, a Ford, and a Faulkner column. I as-
sume that the reader is not the perfect polymath but also that
he does not want to be led by the nose. The book is a study of
three artists together, and the completed study of any one
would violate it even as the perfection of any single discipline's approach will destroy the interdisciplinary. I think it
does address some important general issues of evaluation. I try
to understand as much of American art as can be dealt with
under my self-imposed limitations: what can we know of the
relationships between artists' canons and the genres so crucial
to American art, what can we understand of the way those
canons and these particular artists treat a great American

idea, community? What can the work of these three tell us about genre itself?

Jon Barlow and I had good students in American Studies 282 and English 227; I thank them all. Some of those who made particular contributions to this book were James Fairbrother ('77), Leah Schmidt ('77), and Adam Usdan ('83). Adam Levy ('85) verified, researched, and helped me for a summer. Kit Reed provided the title and is the chief collaborator in my continuing informal attempt to understand narrative. Nicolas Collins and I assisted Barlow in recording Ives's songs and keyboard music, and I learned from him about music. Katy Reed worked on the index.

"Canon" is revised from its first appearance (January 1980) in *Faulkner Studies 1*, pp. 136–51. "Community" grew from a lecture in India on a State Department and USIS lecture tour under the Visiting Speakers program (1974) and from a piece delivered at the invitation of the Faulkner Seminar of the New England Modern Language Association in Toronto (1981). Some conversations with Jan G. Deutsch of the Yale Law School were very useful to this piece. I offered the finished chapter as a tribute to David E. Swift of the Wesleyan Religion Department. George R. Creeger contributed to this and other chapters. "Genre" grew out of a long-term faculty seminar with my colleagues in Film and American Studies Jeanine Basinger and Richard S. Slotkin. The seminar was supported more than once by Wesleyan faculty-project grants and faculty-research grants, as I have been again and again supported by these colleagues' knowledge, wit, and reflections. Jon Barlow's teaching, argument, talk, and research inform the whole book: without him I could never have known Ives. Wesleyan's generous sabbatical and leave programs have made writing possible. Adair Bather, Janice Guarino, and Helen Zawisa have typed several versions. Edward Rubacha has sought out references. Joan Jurale has answered specific queries, as she has for most of my scholarly career. Jeannette Hopkins is a splendid editor. I am indebted to John Belton, Stanley Cavell, Alvin C. Kibel, Robert F. Lucid, and Phyllis Rose for timely readings, to Paul Horgan for a reading and a consultation, and to D. P. Moynihan for some very early encouragement.

Middletown, Connecticut, August 1983

FORD, FAULKNER, AND IVES:
AN INTEGRATED CHRONOLOGY

Adapted in shortened form from chronologies in Joseph
Blotner, *Faulkner: a Biography*, II: 218–21; Peter Bogdanovich, *John Ford*, pp. 109–44; *Charles E. Ives Memos*, ed.
John Kirkpatrick, pp. 325–37. The number following each
artist's initials (WF, JF, CI) indicates his age in that year.

		20 Oct. 1874
CI		born Danbury, Ct. to George Edward Ives and Mary Elizabeth Parmelee
		1881
CI 7		attends New Street School, Danbury
		1887
CI 13		plays *As Pants the Hart* (?composed by him) at Methodist Church; first sketch of *Slow March*; *Holiday Quick Step*
		1888
CI 14		engaged as supply organist
		1889
CI 15		organist, Second Congregational Church
		1892
CI 18		plays *America Variations* at Brewster, N.Y.
		1893
CI 19		enrolls at Hopkins Grammar School, New Haven; organist, St. Thomas Church, Center Church, New Haven
		1895
CI 21		"finishes" *First Symphony*
		1 Feb.
	JF	born Sean Aloysius Feeney, Cape Eliza- beth, Me. to Sean Feeney and Barbara Curran, who had come separately to America from Ireland; moves to Portland

		25 Sept. 1897
	WF	born, New Albany, Miss., to Murry Cuthbert Falkner and Maud Butler
		1898
CI 24		earns BA at Yale; begins work with Mutual Life Insurance Company
		1901
CI 27		"finishes" *Second Symphony*; begins *Third Symphony* and *First Piano Sonata*
		1903
CI 28		begins *Violin Sonatas*
		1905
	WF 8	attends Oxford Graded School
CI 31		*Three-Page Sonata*
		1906
CI 32		*Halloween*
		1908
CI 34		marries Harmony Twichell
		1909
	WF 12	works in father's livery stable
CI 35		Ives & Myrick, insurance brokers, established
		1911
CI 37		first idea for *Concord Sonata*, Sept.; *Hawthorne*, Oct.
		1912
CI 38		*Emerson*; buys 14½ acres in Redding, Ct., "no buildings"; *The St.-Gaudens in Boston Common*
		1913
	JF 18	graduates Portland High School; goes to Hollywood and gets job with brother Francis; begins as stunt man and general laborer

1914

WF 17   beginning of friendship with Phil Stone

JF 19   works as writer, actor, stuntman for films; directed by Francis Ford and others (including Griffith in *Birth of a Nation*, playing a member of the Klan); listed as director for *Lucile the Waitress*, a series of four two-reelers, but no print survives and JF remembered nothing of it

CI 40   plays *Emerson* at church concert in New York; "finishes" *Fourth Symphony*; *General William Booth*; *The Alcotts*

1915

WF 18   goes bear-hunting at "General" James Stone's camp

1916

WF 19   bookkeeper at First National Bank, Oxford; writes verse

JF 21   listed as "Jack Ford, assistant director" in *Motion Picture News* Studio Directory

1917

JF 22   wrote and directed *The Tornado* (2 reels) (JF: "just a bunch of stunts"); *The Soul-Herder*, the first of twenty-five silent films with Harry Carey; *Straight Shooting*, Ford's first feature; and five more films

CI 43   *He Is There!*

1918

WF 21   joins Phil Stone in New Haven; ledger clerk, Winchester Repeating Arms Co.; accepted by Royal Canadian Air Force as cadet; trains in Canada; discharged early Dec.

JF 23   seven films

CI 44   "Charlie taken sick . . . out of business all winter"

1919

WF 22   poem, "L'Après-Midi d'un Faune," appears in *New Republic*; enters U. of Miss. as special student

JF 24   fifteen films, including *The Outcasts of Poker Flat*

1920

WF 23   withdraws from university; hand-letters six copies of *Marionettes*, verse play

JF 25   five films, including one starring "Gentleman Jim" Corbett; meets and marries Mary McBryde Smith

1921

WF 24   accepts Stark Young's invitation to visit New York; works as bookstore clerk and lives in Greenwich Village; returns to Oxford as postmaster at University Post Office, Dec.

JF 26   seven films; son Patrick born

CI 47   Schirmer completes printing of *Concord Sonata*; CI returns to business

1922

WF 25   becomes scoutmaster

JF 27   three films, including *Little Miss Smiles*; daughter Barbara born

CI 48   Schirmer ships galley proofs for *114 Songs*; reviewed in Aug.

1923

JF 28   five films, including *Cameo Kirby* with John Gilbert and two starring Tom Mix

1924

WF 27   fired as scoutmaster for drinking; resigns from post office after postal inspector brings charges; meets Sherwood Anderson; is paid $400 for *The Marble Faun*

JF 29   *The Iron Horse*

1925
WF 28   trip to Europe

1926
WF 29   *Soldiers' Pay*
JF 31   *Three Bad Men*
CI 52   *Sunrise*, apparently Ives's last composition

1927
WF 30   *Mosquitoes*
CI 53   Goossens conducts part of *Fourth Symphony*, Town Hall, New York City

1928
JF 33   *Napoleon's Barber*, a 32-minute talkie
CI 54   Oscar Ziegler plays *The Alcotts* (*Concord Sonata*, III) at Salzburg

1929
WF 32   *Sartoris*, Jan.; marries Estelle Lida Oldham as second husband (her first marriage, to Cornell Franklin, ended in divorce); works at university power plant; *The Sound and the Fury*, Oct.
JF 34   *The Black Watch*, JF's first talkie feature
CI 55   *Fourth Symphony* published in *New Music*

1930
WF 33   purchases and names Rowan Oak; *As I Lay Dying*; "A Rose for Emily," his first short story, published
JF 35   *Men Without Women*
CI 56   retires from Ives & Myrick; Slonimsky conducts *Three Places in New England* for I.S.C.M. Committee

1931
WF 34   daughter born, lives nine days; *Sanctuary*, Feb., *These 13* (short stories), Sept.
JF 36   *Arrowsmith*
CI 57   Ives hears Slonimsky conduct *Three*

		Places; Slonimsky conducts *Three Places in Boston*; CI decides to write *Memos*
		1932
	WF 35	goes to work as contract writer at MGM, May–Aug.; *Light in August*, Oct.
	JF 37	*Air Mail*, based on book by Frank "Spig" Wead
		1933
	WF 36	daughter, Jill, born
CI 59		34 songs in *New Music*
		1934
	WF 37	writes for Universal
	JF 39	*The Lost Patrol*; *Judge Priest*
		1935
	WF 38	writes for Twentieth Century–Fox; *Pylon*
	JF 40	*The Informer* wins New York Film Critics Award, best-director Academy Award, and three other Oscars
CI 60		18 [19] songs in *New Music*
		1936
	WF 39	*Absalom, Absalom!*
	JF 41	*Prisoner of Shark Island*
		1937
	JF 42	*Wee Willie Winkie*; *The Hurricane*
		1938
	WF 41	*The Unvanquished*, sold to MGM
CI 64		John Kirkpatrick plays *Concord Sonata* at Cos Cob
		1939
	WF 42	elected to National Institute of Arts and Letters; *The Wild Palms*
	JF 44	*Stagecoach* (JF director-producer; first film shot in Monument Valley; wins New York Film Critics Award; Oscars, but none to JF); *Young Mr. Lincoln*; *Drums Along the Mohawk*

CI 65   Kirkpatrick plays *Concord Sonata* at Town Hall; Gilman's review: "the greatest music composed by an American"

1940

WF 43   *The Hamlet*

JF 45   *The Grapes of Wrath*, Academy Award for best direction and to Jane Darwell; New York Film Critics Award for this and, in same year, *The Long Voyage Home*

CI 66   Babitz and Dahl play *Third Violin Sonata* at Los Angeles

1941

JF 46   *How Green Was My Valley*, Academy Award for best direction and best production, three others; New York Film Critics Award for direction; active duty, U.S. Navy; appointed Chief, Field Photographic Branch, Office of Strategic Services, to head the unit he organized "to photograph . . . the work of guerillas, saboteurs, Resistance outfits. . . . [and] special assignments"

1942

WF 45   *Go Down, Moses*; writes for Warners on long-term contract, continuing into 1945: *To Have and Have Not* (released 1944) and *The Big Sleep* (released 1946)

JF 47   *The Battle of Midway*, the first U.S. wartime documentary, 20 mins.; *December 7th*, 20 mins., criticized by War Department, censored, and cut; shoots films in Burma and Yugoslavia

1943

CI 69   records ten sides at Mary Howard's studio

1945

JF 50   *They Were Expendable*

CI 71   Kirkpatrick records *Concord Sonata* at Columbia Records (issued 1948)

1946

WF 49   *The Portable Faulkner*, ed. Malcolm
Cowley

JF 51   *My Darling Clementine*

CI 72   Lou Harrison conducts *Third Symphony*,
Carnegie Chamber Music Hall

1947

JF 52   *The Fugitive*

CI 73   Pulitzer Prize (*Third Symphony*)

1948

WF 51   *Intruder in the Dust*, sold to MGM;
elected to American Academy

JF 53   *Fort Apache*; *Three Godfathers*

1949

JF 54   *She Wore a Yellow Ribbon*

CI 75   William Masselos plays *First Piano Sonata*
at YMHA, New York

1950

WF 53   awarded American Academy's Howells
Medal for fiction (*Collected Stories*);
Nobel Prize for Literature

JF 55   *Wagon Master*; *Rio Grande*

1951

WF 54   National Book Award (*Collected Stories*);
Requiem for a Nun published and play
produced; Legion of Honor

JF 56   *What Price Glory?*

1953

WF 56   writes for Howard Hawks, *Land of the
Pharaohs* (released 1955)

JF 58   *Mogambo*

CI 79   Charles Ives program at Jonathan
Edwards College, Yale

1954

WF 57   *A Fable*; International Writers' Conference, Saõ Paulo, Brazil

		19 May
CI		dies, New York
		1955
	WF 58	National Book Award, Pulitzer Prize (*A Fable*); State Department trip to Japan (*Faulkner at Nagano*, 1956)
JF 60		*The Long Gray Line*, JF's first film in Cinemascope
		1956
JF 61		*The Searchers*
		1957
	WF 60	Writer-in-Residence, U. Va. (*Faulkner in the University*, 1959); Silver Medal of the Greek Academy; *The Town*
		1959
	WF 62	*The Mansion*
JF 64		*The Horse Soldiers*
		1960
	WF 63	appointed to U. Va. faculty
		1961
	WF 64	State Department trip to Venezuela
JF 66		*Two Rode Together*
		1962
	WF 65	visits U.S. Military Academy (*Faulkner at West Point*, 1969); Gold Medal for Fiction of National Institute of Arts and Letters; *The Reivers*, 4 June; injured in fall from horse, 17 June; dies at Oxford of heart attack, July
JF 67		*The Man Who Shot Liberty Valance*
		1964
JF 69		*Cheyenne Autumn*
		1966
JF 71		*Seven Women*

1972

JF 77   Life Achievement Award (the first
             given) of American Film Institute

1973

JF 78   awarded Presidential Medal of Freedom;
             dies, Palm Desert, Ca., 31 Aug.

IN THE AMERICAN GRAIN

This is a book about America and three artists who worked there. America is a popular subject matter for generalizers: everybody has always been able to pronounce on the character of the Americans for very good reason—Americans have never kept it to themselves. But hidden within these generalizations, concealed by the readiness of cliché, there are some truths worth detailing because they bear upon the artists at hand, not so much upon what they were as Americans—whether they were "good" Americans or "proper" American artists—but what they had to appear to be in order to be artists in America, what they couldn't afford to look as if they were doing, and what they really thought they were doing—behind all these multiple cover stories. These masks and disguises are important: sometimes they can serve as faces.

Americans are ambivalent. They judge ambivalently. Any one of them would punch you up if you suggested this was true about *him*, but this, of course, only confirms that it is true. Any one of them would like to call this ambivalence a sense of fairness. Any firm adjective of self-analysis will be followed by an "on the other hand" or "but" and then claim the contrary quality, some qualification. This leads to something like a prior denial of the possibility of characterization itself and this in turn ("Well, you can't really say that . . .") leads to sudden blurted affirmations. Characterization becomes denial plus boast: prior negation, later hyperbole. Americans like to claim more than their due, but to claim it modestly and to act as if no claim is being made. This leads to the excesses and deviousness of American advertising, leads to the Great White Fleet of the early twentieth century, to Showing the Flag, and to what Americans blithely interpret as pushing around other people or nations for their own good. When Teddy Roosevelt admonished Americans to speak softly and carry a Big Stick, his admonition defined him and other Americans.

It also leads to American adoption and assimilation (as if *we* had thought it up to begin with) of the most violent and vituperative criticism from abroad. G. K. Chesterton says,

"Most Americans are born drunk. . . . They have a sort of permanent intoxication from within,"[1] and we take it as an interior effervescence. Kipling adds, "Enslaved, illogical, elate,/ He greets the embarrassed Gods, nor fears/ To shake the iron hand of Fate/ Or match with Destiny for beers,"[2] and the American thinks himself a good sport out on the town. Shaw put his finger on the way in which Americans seem to collaborate in the world's regret of them: "To house their eager interest, their distinguished consideration, and their undying devotion, all that is necessary is to hold them up to the ridicule of the rest of the universe. Dickens won them to him forever by merciless projections of typical Americans as windbags, swindlers, and assassins."[3] Clever Americans saw this as a way of turning away rejection and criticism, a way to survive the blows. Mark Twain added a characteristic understatement, really a better weapon than Thomas Carlyle's barb to which it responded, "He was probably fond of them, but he was always able to conceal it."[4]

There is in Americans (along with the ambivalence) the love of disguise or mask. The mask we like best is the poker player's bluff, impassive for good reason and for profit, not for the sake of distance or imperviousness. "When you call me that, *smile*," says Owen Wister's Virginian.[5] We want to get something out of getting dressed up.

So Americans like to best the opponent, to get the better of a deal, to be able to lick anybody on the street, or at least have a father who can—but to be able to do so without looking important or rich or powerful or strong—to *be* better, but to be no *better* than anyone on the street. This need to *be* better is connected with know-how, the mind's equivalent, I suppose, of the Big Stick—in any event, a blunt instrument. Know-how (as in "he sure does know his stuff") is to be sought only if it never touches the books: book learning is wrong (or must be denied) because it's effete and not practical. We have to acquire know-how ourselves, street smarts instead of book learning. The Virginian "had been equal to the situation. That is

the only kind of equality which I recognize."[6] Alexis de Tocqueville characterizes this as a faith in the Cartesian method:
"Of all countries in the world, America is the one in which
the precepts of Descartes are least studied and best followed
. . . to escape from imposed problems . . . , to seek for oneself in oneself for the only reason for things."[7] Michael Paul
Rogin adds that this creates a vacuum between the scientist
and the romantic artist, with the mode of either scientist or
artist being of little use for understanding the body social.[8]
Another, rather impatient, statement of hope that Americans
might improve a little in the knowledge category was, un-
characteristically, from Ralph Waldo Emerson: "I hate this
shallow Americanism which hopes to get rich by credit, to get
knowledge by raps on midnight tables, to learn the economy
of the mind by phrenology, or skill without study, or mastery
without apprenticeship."[9]

The American prides himself on being what he calls Natural (Edmund Spenser's Salvage Man, who shows up in the
later books of *The Faerie Queene* and goes about bopping people, is an Ur-American), a man who knows but the book of
nature, reads it aright, gets his know-how by the Mountain
Man's closeness to the land, and applies it to any practical
problem at hand. "Stories of savage men and uncouth manners," says Burke, with which America will still "show itself
equal to the whole of that commerce which now attracts the
envy of the world."[10] Or "perhaps a Thucydides at Boston,"
writes Horace Walpole, "a Xenophon at New York."[11]

One of Thomas Eakins's most eloquent theoretical statements is set in a natural metaphor:

The big artist does not sit down monkey like and copy a coal scut-
tle or an ugly old woman like some Dutch painters have done not a
dung pile, but he keeps a sharp eye on Nature and steals her tools.
He learns what she does with light the big tool and then color then
form and appropriates them to his own use. Then he's got a canoe of
his own smaller than Nature's but big enough for every purpose except to paint the midday sun which is not beautiful at all. It is plenty

strong enough though to make midday sunlight or the setting sun if
you known how to handle it. With this canoe he can sail parallel to
Nature's sailing. He will soon be sailing only where he wants to selecting nice little coves and shady shores or storms to his own liking,
but if he ever thinks he can sail another fashion from Nature or
make a better shaped boat he'll capsize or stick in the mud and nobody will buy his pictures or sail with him in his old tub.[12]

Eakins like a good American sailed and skated. The city then
still met the land. Ives found an absolute good in the "substance" this added to music. "We might offer the suggestion
that Debussy's content would have been worthier his manner
if he had hoed corn or sold newspapers for a living, for in this
way he might have gained a deeper vitality and a truer theme
to sing at night and of a Sunday."[13] For him the "natural"
was part of a system coherent with republican simplicity and
democratic tasks: man without adornment. Rousseau would
have been proud of him, as he would have been proud of us
Americans if he'd seen how we turned out, and as proper god-
father he would have had some claim to his pride. But the
natural vein apparently has more force in metaphor than in
planning. Americans (on the other hand) invented urban
blight and suburban sprawl.

Americans like to be on the move, to be moving, to get
away, to get on with it, get on to the next thing: "the impres-
sion, that whatever swift, rushing thing I stood on was not so
much bound to any haven ahead as rushing from all havens
astern."[14] The Englishman traveling with P. T. Barnum recorded a wonderful series of conversations with him, with just
about the most characteristic Barnum utterances there are in
print. "'We've none of them old fixings in Amerikey,' Barnum
remarked. 'They've no time to get old there. . . . A man
never builds a house to last above a year or two, because he's
gone-a-head in that time, and wants a bigger one. And go-a-
head is our motto. Shut the firedoor, sit on the safety valve,
and whop the sun.'"[15] The Virginian says he's "the kind that

moves up." The Frontier is dynamic not just because it keeps advancing and changing its leading edge, but because it has this motile vitality of Americans going, on the move, glimpsed only as a blur. The journey is at the center of American literature and the American film (especially of the American Western) as surely as the myth of moving—and the fact of moving inherent in immigration and the several Great American Migrations—is at the center of American history.

The first step was the conquest of nature; the second the conquest of this vast new space. Edward Everett saw the two connected: "The older parts of the country, which have been settled by the husbandman, and reclaimed from the state of nature, are now to be settled again by the manufacturer, the engineer, and the mechanic. First settled by a civilized, they are now to be settled by a dense, population. Settled by the hard labor of the human hands, they are now to be settled by the labor-saving arts, by machinery, by the steam engine, and by internal improvements." [17]

Journeys are at the center of John Ford's *Stagecoach*, *The Hurricane*, *Three Godfathers*, *The Searchers*, *Two Rode Together*, *The Man Who Shot Liberty Valance*, *The Grapes of Wrath*, *Drums Along the Mohawk*, *Wagon Master*, *The Horse Soldiers*, and many more. But perhaps more important is that people in Ford pictures *move* (with certain notable exceptions such as *The Lost Patrol* and *Seven Women*—but they arrive and leave even there); they still move even when it's clear they aren't advancing or journeying anywhere in relation to the monuments of Monument Valley, about which they circle and spiral and wander. All Faulkner's novels start and end in movement (men and women "shown for a moment in a dramatic instant of the furious motion of being alive, that's all any story is. . . . this fluidity which is human life") [18] especially *Light in August*, *Sanctuary*, *As I Lay Dying*. Many of his most telling metaphorical moments (the Sutpen Family's migration in *Absalom, Absalom!*, Benjy in the wagon at the end of *The Sound and the Fury*, Darl and the road as spool of thread in *As I Lay Dying*) turn on movement, motion, getting on with it, getting away. Even Ives, in the more restricted sense in which music can depict, cherishes sounds coming and going away, bands passing, choirs at a distance, sounds of music moving through its space (and ours).

Jeanine Basinger has identified this movement in American films as the essential core, so interchangeable from one genre to the next (Musical, Woman's, Western, Costume, and so on) that it is beyond *story*: the sequence behind the actions every American seems to have to try to recapitulate in order to attempt to replicate in himself the whole of our history: Discovery, Immigration, Colonization, Exploration, Enterprise, Entrepreneurship, and War.[19] And why do we need to make this for ourselves? Even failure cannot be learned out of a book, but has to be tasted, victory savored, experience absorbed, know-how used to become our own, ourselves, ours. I'm (We're) from Missouri.

But also because it's American (it goes with the territory, as Willie Loman would say) to want to belong, to have a piece of the action, have our own Frontier to match the country's big one, to possess objects or pieces of furniture that were moved years ago by Conestoga or ox-cart, to have forebears coming up on the Lower East Side who fled the Cossacks, to discover for ourselves a new land unknown by our parents. That journey seems to figure in the experiences recollected by both hero and citizen alike: wherever elderly Americans gather to reminisce we see it, and it is traced by novels and poems and operas. This motion is the centerpiece of our national experience, partly because we are so involved with it as individuals. The replication in each citizen of his nation's experience is part of the need to be American, and this need is American. It pairs itself with a strong national tendency toward self-determination, the need for anyone American to be himself, to be his own woman or man, the cosmic need for originality. (Davy Crockett's motto was "Be sure you're right, then go ahead.") And once we are original, the cosmos must show, in turn, an overpowering need for *us*—for American enterprise, our go-get-it, our know-how. This goes along with the need to be best but to be no better, and thus paradoxically, with a need to be no different. Thus again our need to remake within ourselves a small America.

The vehicles we use for these journeys take on symbolic force—the Conestoga, the canal and the steamboat, the automobile (locus of one of the most elaborate of all the American romances with its machines because it is so personal), the plane, the space shuttle. The locomotives joining their tracks with a Golden Spike at Promontory Point, Utah, are perhaps the most powerful symbols in this sequence, ambivalent enough to suit the American taste, as the act of joining our spiritual halves emanating from either Coast only affirmed that it was, in Lena Grove's words, "a fur piece," a right fur piece—and probably affirmed as well that never the twain shall meet.

In contrast to Europeans, Americans prefer horses to servants. (But on the other hand how many of our movies involve Americans who have servants, upstairs/downstairs, the *nouveau riche?*—*My Man Godfrey, Love Finds Andy Hardy, Tovarich, Trading Places, Imitation of Life.*) Servants are Old World: wagons and steamboats and machines with wheels (or wings) are tools. And tools are know-how: the Plow That Broke the Plains. (But: then "they were rich enough for a *staff of five.*" And—the biggest *but* in American history—slavery, cause of our most long-lived national agony.) Americans like machines even better than horses. Horses are profoundly involved in Americans' most violent derring-do, but horses are too much like servants, and will be dispensed with when a good machine comes along. The Iron Horse and "Get a Horse" are ambivalent rejections or denials of that once-necessary beast. On the other hand, latter-day derring-do must involve horses to be *echt* derring-do; to have that Last Stand out of due season the horse returns, Pickett Rides, the Seventh Cavalry lives.

Americans like Abraham Lincoln. It's not just because they are told in school that he is their quintessential hero, but because he is so right again and again: he looks the way they'd like to (lanky), does it himself (splits rails), does it right (directly), learns right (by the light of the fire), and knows what he knows right (from experience). He stays simple. His roots are right and he talks about them right. Roots aren't much use unless you talk about them, and talking about them becomes a part of an individual's self-importance, a personal myth of origin as significant to him as a cocked hat or a fingerprint and a little America within each citizen. (Charlie Starkweather and Willie Sutton talked, too; that their tales were different from Lincoln's didn't make them less American, but maybe more so, because theirs were so out of phase with his, in their way frank and original). Lincoln's self-improvement (even though he learned from books) was a model for autodidacts through the ages, do-it-yourself improvement as American as adding an egg (or, in *State Fair*, a little booze) to somebody else's recipe (see Faulkner's improvement on Joyce's stream of consciousness in *The Sound and the Fury*), as endemic as jogging (how many hymn tunes can dance on a single piece by Charles Ives?).

Contrast the George Washington myth of Parson Weems, Old World in many respects because he didn't yet know what would be needed to make this myth American. Lincoln stayed simple. The question of the proper honorific title for a president of the United States would never have come up at all if Lincoln had come before Washington. Contrast Washington of this earlier myth and Lyndon Johnson of a later one, the "simplicity" of the rejection of a crown (Lincoln certainly had the power of a king but never had the chance to reject a crown) and the simplicity of Lyndon's Natural Man—lifting his beagles by their ears or exposing his gall-bladder scar at a press conference. And how those two things worked against him. Like Washington, Lincoln had dignity and knew when he was being funny. Americans like humorists and make them heroes: Mark Twain and Crockett and Will Rogers. It was Lyndon Johnson's failure at *that* that doomed the self-generated Johnson Myth. And Charles Starkweather's and Willie Sutton's mastery of that put the Good Housekeeping Seal of Approval on their own American Myths.

Lincoln's family is perhaps not so American as Lyndon Johnson's, because Americans like to quarrel with their families. There was Mrs. Lincoln, of course, but a good American quarrel is with more than the wife—it's parents with children and brother against brother. The Johnson daughters gave free rein to our imagination to body forth good American quarrels.

While Americans do it by themselves they don't like to be interfered with as they are about it. A student from the People's Republic of China has given us a contrast: "In America you say it's none of my business; in China you say it's none of your business." [20] The younger Little Brother, although he fights the Older Sibling, will want to make it on his own without that help. He will do it alone, but he wants a good woman behind him (not necessarily a wife or a light-of-love, Tom Sawyer's Aunt Polly will do). This much of the myth is of nineteenth-century origin (as so much of it is) and relentlessly male. It may well be that a lot of these ambivalences have origins in the male. But if he can't have one of those good women, he'd rather do it alone. But if he can have one, they did it together. But they did it alone.

For Little Brother, read American; for Older Sibling, read Europe; for quarrel, read the competitiveness of the late eighteenth and early nineteenth centuries—diplomatic, bellicose, entrepreneurial. For mottos seek again Emerson's admonition on the muses. Or "The less America looks abroad, the grander its promise"; or "One day we will cast out the passion for Europe, by the passion for America"; or, finally, the crowing of a triumphant success, "We have learned to forget foreign nations."[21] Or one that raises "new voices" over the tired babble of the (carefully concocted phrase) Old World. For yet another switch on this, run through the lyrics of the popular song of World War II, "We did it before and we can do it again," World War II as street fight, common action as the strength and resolve of/or to defeat a single simple bully. In the immortal observation of Gabby Hayes, even a hardboiled egg can be yellow on the inside.

Emerson threw down the gauntlet, but duels are better fought with the opponents present, which is probably one reason for the long-term sibling rivalry. The need to be American was a need to be compared *right now* to that Elder Sibling (this made the competition respectable, the prize worth the run, worth winning), even as Little Brother bested him. The Frontier brags come in here.

Then I went over to the great arms factory and learned my real trade; learned all there was to it; learned to make everything: guns, revolvers, cannon, boilers, engines, all sorts of labor-saving machinery. Why, I could make anything a body wanted—anything in the world, it didn't make any difference what; and if there wasn't any quick new-fangled way to make a thing, I could invent one—and do it as easy as rolling off a log. . . . One thing at a time, is my motto—and just play that thing for all it is worth, even if it's only two pair and a jack. I made up my mind to two things: if it was still the nineteenth century and I was among lunatics and couldn't get away, I would presently boss that asylum or know the reason why; and if, on the other hand, it was really the sixth century, all right, I didn't want any softer thing: I would boss the whole country inside of three months for I judge I would have the start of the best educated man in the kingdom by a matter of thirteen hundred years and upward.[22]

Frontier brags are paired ambivalently to the whimper of modesty by which the American artist wants to be seen as no better than the man in the street. This kinship to the Common Man is perhaps even more important than the hyperbolic boasts because an American before his fellow Americans is a more significant self-presentation to Americans than an artist before artists. Modesty about prizes (see Faulkner's Nobel Prize Address, a rare mixture of the apparently unsuccessful striving for originality and this peculiarly American false modesty) is one result. Ford liked prizes; Ives did not.

We hear that Mr. Smith or Mr. Morgan, etc., *et al.* design to establish a "course at Rome," to raise the standard of American music, (or the standard of American composers—which is it?); but possibly the more our composer accepts from his patrons "*et al.*," the less he will accept *from himself.* . . . It may be that many men—perhaps some of genius . . . have been started on the downward path of subsidy by trying to write a thousand-dollar prize poem or a ten-thousand-dollar prize opera. How many masterpieces have been prevented from blossoming in this way? . . . If a bishop should offer a "prize living" to the curate who will love God the hardest for fifteen days, whoever gets the prize would love God the least. Such stimulants . . . tend to industrialize art.[23]

But then again, Americans like underdogs and loners and (in spite of that Big Stick) love to pose as the underdogs, so the comparison and the sibling rivalry goes on. "I can too" boasting is mixed with abnegation, so that rivalry with Europe seems even more like our conflicts with our real brothers and sisters, absolutely essential for our self-respect, but absolutely childish. Little Brothers and Sisters are nothing if not that. And in all fairness, so are Big Brothers and Sisters. Barnum again, after he had passed a barber near Stratford named Shakespeare: "Shakespeare—hairdresser—a good shave for a penny":

Now if that Barber was to write a play . . . it wouldn't be thought anything of, however good it was, till he's been dead no end of years. You talk a good deal about your Shakespeare being the pride of England, but I can see nobody knew or cared a cent about him while he was alive, or else you'd have known more of him now. If he'd been a living author, and I'd had my exhibition, I'd have backed General Tom Thumb to have shut him up in a week. [24]

Barnum's emphasis on the finality of judgment that quick profit grants the gainer is American. "Get rich quick" is not just an admonition to beware of fraud: it's also an omnipresent ideal. Sharp trading is American. And characteristic of Little Brothers.

And although we love profit we should prefer not to inherit. In fact, Americans might rather be deprived of an inheritance than get one; like Joseph of the Bible, thinking we're going to get one and then not getting it and then making it ourselves may be the best of both worlds. There has been, of course, a mighty lot of inheritance going on in this country (the counterpart, I suppose, for that stability John Adams yearned for in the inherited dignities and protocol of Europe): the robber barons, the Hudson patroons, the King Ranch. But the purest American pedigree is that belonging to the self-made man or woman. Of course he has siblings. And both failing to inherit and making it on his own are subject to family quarrels with them.

The childhood/sibling metaphor is pervasive. "America is a country of young men"; "A people who are still . . . but in the gristle, and not yet hardened into the bone of manhood"; "The youth of America is their oldest tradition. It has been going on now for three hundred years"; "America is the only place where man is full-grown!"; "Woman governs America because America is a land of boys who refuse to grow up." [25]

Such ambivalence might seem to suit our work better than it does our art. Art is effete, hung up on books, prefers the visionary to the practical, likes inheritance in its methods, its allusions, its tradition, favors the approval of the cognoscenti to that of the man in the street—would from him (on the whole) just as soon have jeers. But there never seems, even in the earliest days, to have been much doubt that for a new country eager to make its mark, art was essential. Maybe America's art had more to do with machines than Europe's did. Maybe talk about art and artists was fated always to be more ambivalent in America even than talk about work or self. But until it had art—or a full set of arts (Emerson called for music, eloquence, poetry, painting, sculpture, architecture[26])—it couldn't claim shape or self *or* independence.

The practical/visionary ambivalence comes, I suppose, with the territory (New Found Land). The Puritans saw two countries and both for them were equally tangible, but the invisible landscape was visionary, the other was practical. Melville's sea yarns started out as practical, then yearned for the visionary. Hawthorne's bad dreams were visionary, yearning to find some sanction for their visions in something more practical: the curse and the photographer of *The House of the Seven Gables*, the Custom House and the vision of Little Pearl in *The Scarlet Letter*.

There was ambivalence in the plain Puritan garb and Hester Prynne's overembroidered badge. Americans have always preferred a severity of line in narrative: true republican architecture, devoid of a show of luxury, massively solid, simple, graceful. The Commissioners for the design of the White House set forth a clear ideal as they recruited Bordeaux craftsmen to work in the new city: they looked for "a grandeur of conception, a republican simplicity, excluding frivolity, that food of little minds."[27] Washington, accepting the gift of a chimney-piece, said on accepting it he feared "for his republican stile of living."[28] In other words, not only was it kingly for him to accept it but the mantel was a bit fancy, so he could flatter the donor (luxurious gift) and himself (modest principles) at the same time.

Plain and fancy is storekeeper's lingo for a split which runs through life and art: when it comes to art the question gets tougher even than it is for life. "I just try to drive the nails

straight so the cabinet comes out right. . . . I write about people. Maybe all sorts of symbols and images get in—I don't
know. When a good carpenter builds something, he puts the
nails where they belong. Maybe they make a fancy pattern
when he's through, but that's not why he put them in that
way." [29] Essentials are practical; decoration lacks this sanction.
Faulkner is happier when he can look as if simplicity is a need
rather than a want. The cover story he concocts for the way
he has made *As I Lay Dying* is an example:

> That's a simple *tour de force*. I took this family and subjected them to
> the two greatest catastrophes which man can suffer—flood and fire,
> that's all. [30]

> Something like *As I Lay Dying* was easy, real easy. A *tour de force*. It
> took me just about six weeks (With a grin). I could write a book like
> that with both hands tied behind my back. It just came all of a piece
> with no work on my part. Just came like that. I just thought of all
> the natural catastrophes that could happen to a family and let them
> all happen. [31]

Faulkner brags. But where *it* comes from must be simple to
be American. But on the other hand the spectre of Europe is
never really very far away. "It may be possible that a month in
a 'Kansas wheat field' will do more for [a composer] than three
years in Rome." [32]

There is a counterpart to this simplicity of origins in development in which tinkering is opposed to the thunderbolt: tugging and nagging at a piece to make it come right is contrasted
to the work of art as Road-to-Damascus. The motto for this
ambivalence is provided of course by Thomas Edison: genius
is one percent inspiration and ninety-nine percent perspira-
tion. What Faulkner finds for an "on the other hand" to
counter *As I Lay Dying*'s simple thunderbolt is the spun-out
agony of trying to finish *The Sound and the Fury*.

> It was going to be a story of blood gone bad. The story told wasn't
> all. The idiot child had started out as a simple prop at first as a bid

for extra sympathy. Then I thought what would the story be told like as he saw it. So I had him look at it. When I'd finished I had a quarter of the book written, but it still wasn't all. It still wasn't enough. So then Quentin told the story as he saw it and it still wasn't enough. Then Jason told the story and it still was not enough, and so I wrote the appendix and it wasn't enough. It's the book I feel tenderest towards. I couldn't leave it alone, and I never could tell it right, though I tried hard and would like to try again though I'd probably fail again. It's the tragedy of two lost women: Caddy and her daughter.[33]

That last sentence is added as emotional coda, enforcement for the frustrations (and stunning results) of tinkering. *Tour de force* has the virtue of simplicity but (by Faulkner's implication) lacks the depth of uncertainty and the tragedy of difficulty or failure. The tougher it is the more it enforces the tinkerer's pattern and routine, just as the more striking the initial inspiration, the more it has of primal force.

Ives tinkered throughout his creative life, but after 1926 had, apparently, no thunderbolts. Some of the songs look as if they could have come on him suddenly, but none of the piano scores do—*First Piano Sonata* is a treasure-trove dig of tinkerer's hen tracks, built up over decades, layered like the Troy Site. Ives's primary metaphor was that of the tinkerer; only in the Golden Age to come would thunderbolts predominate.

The instinctive and progressive interest of every man in art, we are willing to affirm with no qualification, will go on and on, ever fulfilling hopes, ever building new ones, ever opening new horizons, until the day will come when every man while digging his potatoes will breathe his own Epics, his own Symphonies (operas if he likes it); and as he sits of an evening in his back-yard and shirt sleeves smoking his pipe and watching his brave children in *their* fun of building *their* themes, for *their* sonatas of *their* life, he will look up over the mountains and see his visions, in their reality,—will hear the transcendental strains of the day's symphony, resounding in their many choirs, and in all their perfection, through the west wind and the tree tops![34]

It's not clear from this whether Ives thinks the Infants are building up sonatas in their heads while digging their potatoes, Wordsworth fashion, or whether they can "breathe" them out right now.

Some of the desire in American artists to be tinkerers rather than geniuses is falsely apologetic, "republican principle" again: to claim that they did it because they are artists is not wholly American (even though to claim we did it before and we can do it again *is* American). The ambivalence is confusing enough to make one's head spin, but it leads to something rather hangdog in American artists' public statements that we still seem not to have gotten over.

Ford incorporates the metaphor into a different structure: the career is tinkering and individual instances—moments, whole movies—can be thunderbolts of a rather mundane sort: I did it this way because it seemed right at the time; I didn't mean anything by it, that's just how a War picture is done. I was just making a Western. That's just how we did the score. The product is a matter more of professional competence (know-how) and unvisionary practicality (getting the job done, perfecting it) than of voices from above or beyond.

Europeans have a romantic myth of genius: it wells up like a spring within the man and then he creates as a god might— Keats's "godlike hardship." Only Americans would emphasize the *invention* of art—emphasize the tinkerer's work over godlike myth. Emerson uses the metaphor oddly: "In America, the geography is sublime, but men are not; the inventions are excellent but the inventors one is sometimes ashamed of."[35] This may summarize something about that hangdog mode. In general the American democratizes the artist—"He would be a democrat to all above; look how he lords it over all below."[36] This has implications for the matter of who owns the artist as well as who the artist thinks he is and where he stands in the ultimate Scheme of Things. (On the other hand, it just came all of a sudden can sound a lot like a child trying to explain how the candy dish got broken.)

The European issue of genius raises another element of mundane competence, preoccupation with obsessive theme or subject matter or content. Faulkner's prose, by pretty general agreement, is obsessive, but his dialogue or comedy or subject matter (even in *Light in August*, that novel of multiple obsessions) takes its character from the mundane. Ives's use of hymn tune, popular song, patriotic song, anthem, the motival units of tune and the B-A-C-H theme is obsessive as he works through inversion, reversal, the obverse of this or that motif, almost as if he's afraid he's missed one. But his myth of composition, as evidently a great deal of his composition itself, is from the mundane side, produced by the tinkerer. Ford's themes were so obsessive that even an inattentive moviegoer or daily reviewer of the Thirties or Forties caught on: themes of search and disillusionment, collective weal and individual need, dance and massacre, identity and belonging. Yet the medium could not appropriately be described as obsessive, and called so little attention to itself that it had to wait for the Sixties to begin to get critical attention. Everybody knew he was a great director, but nobody, apparently, tried to deal with it critically because he was so clearly popular.

All this is matched elsewhere in the American Grain: Jackson Pollock dripped as the most mundane housepainter dripped, dripped obsessively but never dripped *like* the housepainter. Alexander Calder, with his obsession with weight and movement in the mobiles, then with weight and stability in the stabiles, nevertheless pursued his art in bits and pieces, mundane circus figures, toys, and junk. Or take a native tradition, the American stonecutters' versions of British tombstone themes scratched and scraped on different stone in the different air of New England: brownstone and slate surfaces were mundane (and surely the occasion death provided for the images); the images were transcendent.

To list more and more ambivalences is possible, but now we get to some difficult overlapping areas where ambivalences cross each other and merge and run together like so many water colors: the ambivalence between drawing the moral (as opposed to letting the work tell its own story, moralize itself); Americans are kind, open, and generous and want to share (we dug it, we paid for it, it's ours). Americans do it better, will perfect it when others fail (there's one born every minute, any damn thing will sell if it's promoted right). It is possible, of course, with so many ambivalences to assert that even figures most apparently distant from the center of American art will fit somewhere in the American Grain if the model is described by such pairings of opposed qualities.

But to the model I have set up these three artists are especially apt. Faulkner, Ford, and Ives have odd grounds in common in the American Grain and in the way they handle suspension, absolutely essential to what *they* seem to have thought they were doing. All three cherish suspension, the last element of ambivalence we must discuss: how all this swinging between opposites can be rationalized.

That "on the other hand" and "but" of the Americans—the switching-stations that lie between one epithet and its opposite in ambivalence—provide balance points. But Americans don't want to be at a balance point because they want so to be on the move. Rather they see themselves being at midpoint in a swing between the two, always in motion from one to the other, something like Addie Bundren's description of words in *As I Lay Dying*, "that we had to use one another by words like spiders dangling by their mouths from a beam, swinging and twisting and never touching."[37] The Americans swing between any two qualities, any two adjectival epithets, and the suspension in that tethered movement allows for uncertainty of identity, the process of suspension which appeals not just to the Americans' mercurial, but to their mystical natures: in the process and movement they are mercurial, sliding between generous and grasping; in suspension, mystical, between the spiritual noble savage and the crafty sharper.

Take for a moment that simple hymn which forms a junction in the work of Faulkner, Ford, and Ives, *Shall We Gather at the River?* We gather at the river in order to cross, but we do not cross until we have gathered. If the river is Jordan, this side is life and the other side is the Other Side; gathering is the assembly of Christian sisters and brothers to await the crossing. Or at a funeral (as Ford uses the hymn) we the living gather when one of us has crossed, to look at the river and what lies beyond. "A fur piece," says Lena Grove; Darl is wordier: "Before us the thick dark current runs. It talks up to us in a murmur become ceaseless and myriad, the yellow dimpled monstrously into fading swirls travelling along the surface for an instant, silent, impermanent and profoundly significant, as though just beneath the surface something huge and alive waked for a moment of lazy alertness out of and into light slumber again."[38] We look and hesitate, wonder, stare, rest in our gathering at the edge, in suspension for this moment from our lives, suspended by gathering and by the nature of this edge of living, not yet taken by dispersal, gathering's opposite, and not yet caught up in crossing, gathering's ultimate end. Suspended and in motion. Caught in that furious motion, for the moment, of being alive.

Suspension is all when it comes to ambivalence. For these artists it is even more: it is at the center of their art. Suspended judgment—why they choose to make this particular thing into art—suspended action in film and fiction, suspended progress in music, suspended melody and sequence and image, and the combination resulting in art's suspended meaning. The suspension of gesture which constitutes that pause, so telling, that hesitation at the edge of the next movement. Faulkner, Ford, and Ives invite us: Yes, we will gather at the river.

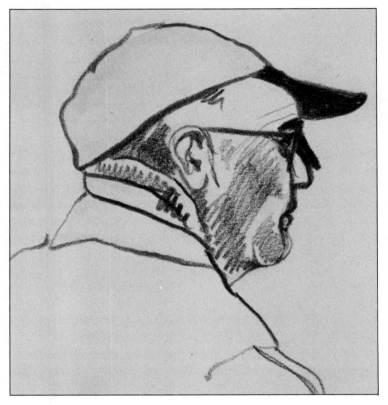

ONE

ORIGINALS

William Faulkner was a man in search of a talent.[1] His early life has little consistency—bum jobs, dropouts, halfhearted respectability, and fitful travel. Poetry as an aim comes in and out of focus and it takes rejection of, flirtation with, and abandonment of an education (to say nothing of a World War) to bring him around to the fiction which becomes his life's work.

His great-grandfather William Clark Falkner (1825–89) was an aristocrat, or at least wanted to act as if he were, as much as his son and grandson and great-grandson did. He was a railroad promoter and was shot down and killed on the street. His grandson Murry (Faulkner's father) was shot in a bar and survived. This could pass for the aristocratic code only in the distorted set of cultural priorities of late-eighteenth-century France or the late-nineteenth-century South, that set of strange needs and drives Faulkner's fiction would eventually integrate into the American Dream.

Faulkner drops out of high school, is tempted back by football, breaks his nose, quits for good. He enlists in the Canadian RAF, returns to the University of Mississippi, writes and publishes poems, joins a fraternity (Sigma Alpha Epsilon). In all this there's something of arrested development, as if not only can he not decide what he's finally going to end up doing, but he cannot get the order and priority of it all straightened out. Fired as scoutmaster and run out of his job as college postmaster by a postal inspector, he starts writing newspaper pieces in New Orleans, finds some sense of direction in the words of Sherwood Anderson, who encourages him to begin to submit fiction to publishers—just as long as Anderson doesn't have to read it first.

He wanders Europe and submissions start to pay off, the career begins to fall into place, but the wandering and something of the fitfulness of back-and-forth never really end. He has a wife and a daughter and a house to which he gives a proper Mississippi name—and a job at the university power plant. Hollywood, whose siren call is blamed for distracting him from his fiction will prove a solid godsend. It provides not only something of a financial constant, but a nearly constant geographical alternative to Mississippi. He was a bit disorganized even among that latter-day Lost Generation of writers at the Polo Lounge and regular screenwriting assignments provided regular periods to his up till now rather accidental and inconsistent progress. There is respectability in writing for Universal, for MGM and Warners in spite of what the snobs say: when the movies twice buy his novels in the year they are published, at least once the money goes for land.

And his reputation as a writer is building at the same time. He is on the cover of *Time* (for his "dirty book" *Sanctuary*, of course). But he drank a bit, like Edmund Wilson, a functioning alcoholic for much of his life. Wilson in his last years could write and drink in the same day, but kept one event rigorously segregated from the other by a scrupulously observed timetable. Faulkner was perhaps not so capable of fine discrimination—binge is more descriptive of the form his dependence takes. Still it does not foster steadiness in the career.

The wandering is of the life and the career and not of the work: the work is much steadier in development and pursued in a far more consistent manner. The most prevalent metaphor for fiction-making Faulkner used in later interviews was that of the apprentice, journeyman, and master carpenter—building a corner, making a shape, squaring a house, finishing a cabinet. Early he wanted to build right, later he taught and preached square building.

After a beginning in rather isolated and emotionally languid verse, Faulkner began to get down to cases with the fictional modes and mannerisms of his day, the lost men and women of World War I and what had happened to them here and abroad. Beneath the fashionable veneer (in *Mosquitoes* and *Soldiers' Pay* veneer seems less metaphorical or a cliché of criticism than a description of fictional method) there were men and women struggling under his journeyman's hands to become, in his words, "flesh-and-blood living people," caught in the furious motion of being alive, but Faulkner's belief in the necessity of Romantic posing and of busy writerliness was keeping them from us as readers. They connect themselves only occasionally to the life that we know and the life that his characters (come *Sartoris*) so convincingly begin to share with us, to breathe our air, to cohabit with us that human condition which seems so whole and complete in Faulkner's best fiction.

The career joined the work in this one sense: Faulkner the loner, the wanderer, wrote from his "sole self" about consciousness to begin with, the ultimate loneliness of fiction. In *The Sound and the Fury, As I Lay Dying*, and in third-person adaptations of consciousness in *Sanctuary* and *Light in August*, he explored the worlds inside individual heads, some of them in pathological states, but all of them working a richly original vein of human privacy until then not really imagined or bodied forth. Later the consciousness of his characters would be forged into a body, become a community, a functioning social structure, as his "little postage-stamp of native soil" became regional and then national epic, one county complete and indivisible, book to book. Even though community would never replace the intensity of Quentin Compson's lonely suffering or Benjy's entrapment, this later work was nevertheless an able medium for something the earlier could not adequately render, Faulkner's sympathy, his kinship with suffering, and the later became an even more efficient medium for our empathy than the earlier had been. For that loss, some gain. Both consciousness and community are a part of the gift of Faulkner's work to us, as surely as form and content go together to make his great world, and the mundane interacts with the experimental to form a seamless whole.

Both career and work are misspoken, perhaps, by this sort of generalized and embalmed ordering. Men don't live by stages, but rather in layers. In the late Twenties and throughout his career into the Sixties Faulkner wrote short stories, both more experimental in method and structure and narrative than the later social novels, and at the same time more social, funnier, and more engaged than the early novels. And there was that continuing series of lesser novels—the *Pylons* and *Knight's Gambits* and *Intruders*—good enough for the career (sometimes preferred to the better novels by the reviewers, the prize-givers, the French), disappointing to the reader's hopes for intensity, for rigor of structure, for experiment in narrative, for that rhythm of his obsessive and by now endearing style.

So there are at least four if not five sequences layered in the work: juvenilia, poetry, and beginnings; early (so-called mainrange) novels of consciousness; the Trilogy and later more social fiction; the short stories; and the in-between books. And at least three if not four careers: wandering uncertainty in odd jobs; going to Hollywood; doing the work, taking the kudos, pontificating, and getting lionized. And one aim: to build it right, or square, or better.

This added up to quite a bit: the most significant body of fictional innovation in American literature, three of its best novels (*As I Lay Dying*, *Light in August*, *The Sound and the Fury*), a consistent land of the national imagination, and prose as unforgettable as any in the language. And as he said, something of the suffering and pettiness and enduring the readers of the country didn't quite know they could manage until they had heard about themselves in his books, a stamp of native soil with meanings emanating from it for the world. An uncertain beginning to certain powerful ends.

He wrote and published and was recognized up to the last months of his life, an active participant in a growing legend, rewriting his apprentice and journeyman experience to fit into the shapes of the now established figure of the lion. Yet not that long before, a small anthology (*The Portable Faulkner*, 1946) resurrected his life's work, almost completely (except for *Sanctuary* and the Modern Library titles) fallen out of print. The back-and-forth continued, apparently, so that, as luck (and achievement) would have it, the second *Time* cover appeared telling of the postage stamp in the terms of distant awe only an Establishment can show for one of its own.

Unlike Faulkner, Ford did not go in search of his talent but of his fortune, as a proper immigrant's son should, to bring over the siblings one by one as the savings mounted.[2] Except that it was his brother who was bringing *him* on: Francis was out there before him in the new land of opportunity, the gold mines of the movies in Hollywood. Ford was born Sean Aloysius Feeney (Ó Fiannaidhe, Ó Fianna, Ó Fidhne) to John A. Feeney, who had been taught his letters in the hedge schools by the priests, sent in 1872 at sixteen to Boston. He moved along to Portland, Maine—the next port to Galway, as it happened—worked for the gas company, married Barbara Curran who had come from across the hill in Galway, and proceeded to become respectable. He and his partners bought one or two saloons or restaurants and became, as saloonkeepers did then, the center for the Irish immigrant community, for politics, for welfare and gossip and news. He became a ward politician, met the young Irish as they came, got them to fill out their citizenship applications, found them jobs.

Ford recalled his father, two uncles—no, four uncles—in the Civil War, which of course had been fought before his father arrived on these shores, trips with his father on that short hop over to Ireland, and the short walk across the hill to home. He remembered that he had learned Gaelic and lost it. So what if none of it was true? It was true belief, and for the American shape which was to form up in his work it was essential prehistory. Later on in his films Ford would make this sort of prehistory stand in for his characters until their actions could take over. The prehistory had a great heritage: immigrants share a common dream and through it write a story in common, with the English or the Cossacks as their villains, with rowings by night and meetings at morning and learning and forgetting. A prehistory in the American Grain.

Ford was born on a farm and wrote that into his script. "I

have kept from my childhood a liking for good people, simple people, people who go on doing their job in the middle of cheats and crooks."[3] And running in the green places of Peak's Island offshore. He saw the Great White Fleet go by in the harbor.

Francis, six years older, had run away to the Spanish-American War and, once fetched home, ran away again to the circus and then to seek his fortune on the stage.[4] Francis had taken Ford as a name (a customary conversion) to hide the stereotypically Irish Feeney. John Ford followed him in name and deed, saw Francis ride by on the screen, then traced his steps to the Promised Land. His bad eyesight kept him out of the navy when he tried to enlist in World War I but did not for a minute delay his rise by means of Hollywood's surrogate for war, the Westerns and Gangsters and Action silents. He fetched and carried, stunted, acted, and became the director Jack Ford. The occasion of the last of these promotions sounds in the telling like more scripting, like those returns to Galway. He was early on the set one morning, sleeping off a drinking bout when Carl Laemmle happened by. Ford on a moment's notice set squads of cowboys to falling off their horses, started a fire on the Western street "more like a pogrom than a Western." Laemmle liked what he saw and set him to directing a Harry Carey Western because he thought "he yells real loud. He'd make a good director."[5] The script was by Ford, constructed in retrospect. But all our scripts have their truth, too. Anybody who could get movement up on the screen could get work then. And Ford yelled loud only until he found more efficient ways of getting his way and getting what he wanted. Then, apparently, his silence was louder than the yells.

Ford couldn't *see* the screen much at all. He had had weak eyes from childhood, wore thick glasses, saw a world only of haze, color, and movement, and was later nearly blind. The eye patch adopted late in life did not cover a missing eye but protected his weaker eye from intense light shifts which are so hard for the pupils of weak or aging eyes to adapt to. And perhaps, as his biographers suggest, the patch acted as his disguise (pirate? renegade? killer? revolutionary?) by which he faced off with associates, particularly actors. He could never see well except in his head but he found a way to get that up on the screen so that when we saw it there on the screen it could make us see; but he had never really seen it through his own eyes at all.

As he went on his vision formed in the combination of image, timing, swiftness of narrative, the subtle pitch of tone, perfected as film followed film, work became whole. This learning process began early, on the Western street. When Ford says one of his early two-reelers was mostly stunts, it is clear stunts would do in that, but he would find a way to make narrative more. And that scripting, which provided him a suitable prehistory, an early life to believe in, served him well as he found himself doctoring the scripts Hollywood handed him. Words on title cards would impede larger action; bits of action could cut them short. Ford would cut out this word and put in that action, connect one part of his film to another by character gesture, narrative jointure, landscape, detailing which was to fill his career with characteristic Fordian moment and hesitation and movement, action emanating from the "flesh-and-blood living people" he made even of the staple cowboys. And that would be accomplished by finding out what could be cut out of the conventional script. Later on it would be told that Ford had answered a studio man's accusation that he was behind schedule by ripping eight pages out of the shooting script. ("You can tell your boss we're back on schedule now," Ford said; and he never shot those pages.[6]) He knew that what came out didn't matter as long as he knew what he was doing. What went in (and it did matter) was Ford.

Harry Carey's character of Cheyenne Harry (from what can be reconstructed from those films, now mostly perished) was a humanization of the hard-riding, quick-shooting *hombre*, and Ford made it in collaboration with Carey out of what he could find in him and make him value. It was to be this analysis and development of an actor's potential, the gradual, careful, and calculating narrowing of the gap between character and actor, that would become Ford's way with performers. Mary Astor's autobiography[7] tells of Ford directing the small Samoan boy of *The Hurricane*, as he told the Governor a lie to protect the escaped Terangi. He would repeat the line ("*Fishing*") for the child, keeping the pitches in the syllables constant, getting the child to repeat after him and calling for takes with hand signals behind his back until he finally got what he wanted: the child just at the edge of nervous fatigue which would read on the screen as the tension of a lie. His work with Wayne and Fonda and Stewart and Marvin and Widmark was, by all reports, similar but subtler. They dimly understood what he was doing—making goats of one or the other of them; at first they resented it, but they never begrudged him his methods once they saw on the screen what he had done. Actors testify to two constants: how well Ford knew them and what a bastard he could seem as he used that understanding to manipulate them, to get them to do one thing more, take it one step farther. In telling about it they would treat this as if Ford knew how to "psych" them out as a coach might. But it seems likely that the true measure of his method was to be found in a collaboration between Ford's expectations and the actors' capabilities as they grew under those expectations of what they might become, when they couldn't see it or dare it or try it themselves. There was a story running around Hollywood about how Ford exploited Victor McLaglen's drunken bouts and hangovers, selecting a performance, the story went, which got on screen Gypo's fogged realization of *The Informer*. Some of this was probably true; it is made cruel in this telling. Afterwards in talking about it actors covered for their stubbornness or humiliation (or even for their self-discovery) by making Ford a bully. But Ford seems never to have sought to justify what he had done by calling *them* inept or clumsy or stupid. He said a few things about actors in general. But not in particular.

He had no doubts for he was always aimed at the movie he knew was there. Ford was badgered by an authenticity-bound assistant, intent on giving Cochise the right smoking equipment for *Fort Apache*: Ford said, "I see him standing against the sky line, one hand clutching his pipe pressed against his chest. . . ." The man on period research recounted the Apaches' use of cigarettes rolled with corn husks, then with Mexican corn paper. Ford listened, and then resumed in the same tones, "I see Cochise, standing straight against the sky line, one hand pressed to his chest . . . and in that hand he may have a flute, he may have an ax, I don't give a damn what he has. . . . But he isn't smoking any cigarette." This anecdote is the story of a man who would brook no obstacle in his way to getting on the screen what he saw inside his head. But it is also the story of a man who knew that the cigarette would be wrong for the myth, wrong for what he was making of the Western. In constructing that great canon of works which his movies together gradually formed, Ford's script for himself stressed the role of the disciplined, practical man intent on getting the job done, not the artist getting his vision or his image right. This persona presents a problem something like the character Geoffrey Chaucer invents to represent himself as one of the pilgrims along for the *Canterbury Tales* pilgrimage: we quickly see that the man in the poem could not write the poem we read; he would not be capable of it. Jack Ford, the happy, partying, bullying, shortcutting, absolute ruler to cast and crew alike, could never have made *The Fugitive* or even *The Informer*, much less *Wagon Master* or *The Hurricane*. The happy pro was a disguise like the eye patch, a false beard for the artist who knew what he wanted and had gradually learned how to get it and then how to get *only* it on the screen.

Coming along at the right time, Ford found in Hollywood not only the pot of gold but the rainbow to go with it. In a world in which you're only as good as your last picture Ford made money and this enabled his art because it kept *them* off his back. They tried, but nobody—not even Goldwyn—interfered with his getting what he called the best picture under the circumstances: "They were thrown at you and then you did the best you could with them."[8] His own script never underestimated the difficulty of getting a movie to look like what he saw inside his head, and he never in that script railed at the failures, the gaps between the job of turning them out and the dream inside his head, because that would have been out of character for the practical, craftsmanlike tinkerer. True, the dream never got nearly enough credit, to hear him tell it. But this was true of all three of these artists in their public statements about what they had done. Ask them about the future of movies or the future of literature or the future of music and you might get that visionary gleam, that utopian light that never was on sea or land. But as to what they had done they could speak only of the practical, the hardheaded, the safely straightforward American work of it.

What Ford did was to invent a lot of America that no one had had the good sense before him to have put into form. He made up genres where there were none, and liberated others to become what they never could have been without his work. He focused our eyes and minds on community, on what was good in us when we were together and what was petty or heroic when we were alone, and vice versa, in ways that now seem downright miraculous but at the time could pass for just real good movies, what movies ought to be, or real troublesome movies, real odd movies, nagging pieces we knew looked like us but which we had to see again and again to be able to understand what we saw ourselves doing in them. He put us together in such a way that afterwards we might recognize what we never saw without his help and what we dared not hope we could be or feared we might become. Because that ideal form his vision sought was generous in its scope: good and bad, virtuous and evil, strong and weak coexisted in measures and balances which never defied the humans we knew. We could believe in them with ease because seen as Ford saw them, they gave us what, once we had learned it the first time, gave us a chance in later films to learn it again and again.

He thought he was making movies and he knew they were pretty good. He denied he was an artist ("Christ," he said, "I hate pictures"), but he knew he was an American and knew he was boss ("I love America. I am apolitical"). He liked silver-studded saddles, military trappings, and large medals from foreign powers. (On his deathbed Ford was asked by Frank Capra if there was anything he could do for him. Ford said yes, he could go to Yugoslavia and stand in for him to get a medal. Capra went.) He was Irish-American, feisty to his enemies and companionable to his fellows, humble before his God and his Church, although he died with a ragtag of shaman sticks and charmed luck-pieces about his neck because he had lived too long and seen too much not to be prepared for some change in the ending.

Charles Ives started his work younger than either of the other two, but then that's possible in music. In literature or film the artist depends on somebody else's money to see into print or onto film what he can do. Of course, Faulkner wrote *Marionettes* and handlettered what he wrote. But I mean to say that Ives's early playing and music were of a piece with what came later. Ives played, it seems, almost before he could reach all the organ's pedals. He was a supply organist at fourteen, playing what seemed to be his own compositions in public at thirteen—not quite a match for Mozart's record, but pretty fair for an American.

The reason he played so is not hard to find. His father, George Ives, was a remarkable musician. Bandmaster to the Danbury, Connecticut Band seems a reduced circumstance for musicianship but if we judge it so we reckon without the spirit of this country just after its greatest agony in the Civil War, and without the spirit of New England, which felt, somehow, it had started all of that and would keep up its fervor with band music. Ives in 1874 was born into that fervor and into his father's unquestioned assumptions about music: that it was an art; that with some adjustments it should be accessible to anyone; that it was essential to the human being and always in the air around him; that sound had a music of its own; that assumptions were made to be questioned, even these.

Perhaps Ives started making music to please his father, but he very quickly started to please himself and never stopped. Eventually he pleased others. It was that next step, pleasing others, that took, as they say in New England, some doing. The accessibility of George Ives's first principles involved the kind of immediacy that the music Establishment would have none of, and a compounding of effects and noises only a Bandmaster would dare to try. Immediacy was hymns sung in church and the organist's embellishments upon them, band music in a bandshell, tunes whistled by anybody. Anyone who cannot sight-read *Slow March* (*114 Songs* No. 114) is no musician, and anyone not moved by it has, in some wise, a tin ear. It is immediate.

This immediacy was Ives's music, the blunt workaday Ives. He was successively organist to several churches in Danbury and New Haven. He played the old stuff and worked out some new. He went from Hopkins Grammar School in New Haven (where he first found his devotion to baseball almost as significant as his devotion to Bach) to Yale and to the teachings of Horatio Parker, straight-arrow oratorio-maker.

The other side, the layering only a bandmaster would dare try, opposite number to the blunt and direct, was planted by George Ives. *America Variations* (which Ives must have played at Center Church on the Green in New Haven) had this, and *The Heavenly Kingdom* had it: a mix or combination resulting from deliberate layering and the accidents which then accrued—a compounding until then unheard of, then unheard for years to come. These pieces also had the direct line, as straightforward as hymns, but they took that odd way to go about it, layer on layer.

Ives had to spell out what he heard in his head. What he strived for was always more direct than he could make it come out on paper for those who were to play his music, wherever they were, and the result was difficult for performers, so alien to what they had learned and strange to contemplate that they labored along, trying to get through what was written down and make it sound right, trying to penetrate scores for music that had seemed, he had thought, so straight in his head. Of course he didn't want it to sound right according to what they had learned, but right to what he wanted. Both the music Establishment and (at first) his performers lacked the faith to try.

It seems likely that it was this faith and the lack of it in others that most troubled Ives. Horatio Parker and his other teachers at Yale must have instilled it: knowledge of a world filled with conservatories, the European courtly muses and Europeanized Rollos (Ives's personification for the music Establishment's lazy taste) behind which American music had to fall in line; knowledge of the "right" ways to go about musical spelling and accompaniment and symphony and sonata construction. Too many conservatories and too many Rollos were to keep performers from seeing what Ives was up to and to make of his life a continuing tacit struggle for public exposure. (But on the other hand, Harmony Ives said to the Cowells, "You know, I have never really liked seeing our name in print."[9])

Ives probably never wanted to make money with his music. Certainly he had determined while at Yale that he must pursue a line of work which would put bread in his mouth rather than try to struggle along picking up lessons and musicmaking. His father's life was, in some regards, not to be emulated. Insurance was burgeoning now and sound as a dollar, and many a dollar Ives & Myrick were to earn at it. He seems never to have doubted that he was in his other career, his art, making the kind of music he wanted to, the music he heard there in his head, but he doubted he could put it across. Probably through this doubt Ives developed the ambivalence of prose (and musical) argument that characterizes not just the essays he wrote to accompany his *114 Songs* when he paid to have them published and (after he had stopped writing music completely) the *Memos*, but also the instructions and notes he attached as players' directions to his scores ("not to be sung"; "t.s.i.a.j. [this scherzo is a joke]").

The difficulty of scoring something that hadn't been on paper before, the apparent irrationality of unheard notes and instruments, of shadow-notes and spirit-notes, of tempi in combat, of reflexive orderings—even of the unperformable—got in the way of performance, although it never touched his music. He wrote one symphony, two, three, four. One immense piano sonata, another. Orchestral sets, chorales, quartets, sonatas for violin and piano. More than one hundred and fourteen songs. Instrumentals, sketches, outlines, ideas. This was directness—this and the occasional concerts sent forth from Poverty Flats where he lived with others starting out on their lives. Wrote it and put it away, the beginning of the collecting process of a lifetime of music he traces so affectingly in the Postface for *114 Songs*: what a musician nails to his dashboard, what is left hanging out on his line.

The muddiness in early performances (some of those that survive on record—never Kirkpatrick's) was inevitable because performers attempted to fit all Ives's music into a Europeanized schema of "right" expectations, make a "whole" out of it. ("A song has a *few* rights the same as other ordinary citizens. If it feels like walking along the left hand side of the street . . . why not let it?")[10] Performers could not let each part seek its own path because they could not believe this was what Ives had wanted. Where no clarity is anticipated, none will show up on its own.

Ives had a heart attack in December of 1918 and stayed out of work for almost a year. The music didn't stop but the energy which had made for a remarkable life of rapid production slackened. In 1926 Ives wrote what is apparently his last com-position, although there was surely tinkering and fussing and adding notes for the rest of his life to the unpublished manu-script pieces.

He remained something of an enigma as he lived on. He was to his secretary the perfect boss, to his wife the perfect husband, to his partner the perfect collaborator in business. This could never have been said of Faulkner or Ford. He lives into 1954 as an object of pilgrimage and still some distant part of the discussion (its object: the discussants saying, He's still there) leading to a consensus that his may indeed be the American music and that it may indeed be performable, or some of it may. There are hero-performers of this time—Kirkpatrick and Slonimsky; Bernard Herrmann, one of Holly-wood's finest writers of film scores, is a champion early and a conductor of late.

It's far easier to evaluate Ives's contribution to the insurance industry (according to Julian Southall Myrick, a lasting gift to that business's way of going about things) than to get at Ives's own contribution to this late-life exploitation and consolida-tion. An icon involved in its own evaluation—to say nothing of worship—would be implicated in some kind of cultural short-circuit. Ives's invalidism and something of the inherent modesty and ambivalence of the 114 Songs Postface argue against this reading.

There was a Pulitzer Prize, entry into the Institute of Arts and Letters, a recording of the Concord Sonata, his most sig-nificant work (recorded six years after and issued nine years after its first performance at Town Hall), the Establishment's scattered, uneasy, and slow acknowledgment that he was there. But always there was something of disconnection. The fact that he still lived was disquieting.

Faulkner and Ford harvest similar rewards late in life, but they are, after all, still producing first-rate work. Ives finally stands as some kind of silent witness beside his work rather than its maker, a somewhat objective witness to the fact that something has again changed the Americans: another blow has been struck in Emerson's cause. His music has changed it and once again Americans are a little bit freer than before, freer of the Older Brother, freer of ourselves. How nice that Ives lived to see it. But the question remains: like the sound of the tree in the Quad, does the candle under the bushel still burn?

TWO

CANON

They do not hold an art in common; they are not of an age or of a single school. Ives is born more than twenty years before either of the other two and has written his last piece of music before either of the others has produced any considerable work. An Irish son of immigrants, a Yankee, a Southerner. Yet as artists somehow alike, not so much in similarities as in affinities—tendencies toward a similar persuasion.

These can be stated in broad terms. There is a social affinity: all three in their lives seem to need to appear to be rather higher on the social scale than they are and at the same time need to appear to have come from the people. There is common to all a general ambivalence of role and image, or character and mask: all are geniuses, but each has his own disguise and wants to use it to temper our temptation to call him a genius: Faulkner must stress that he writes potboilers, Ford must be the efficient Hollywood technocrat, Ives the busy insurance salesman.

Each is a regionalist. Each attends to the past. Each creates a large body of work (even for an American, and they tend to grind it out once they get started), and in each the total output has a structure that could not have been produced by accidental accumulation: the whole work informs the individual works almost more significantly perhaps than parts build a whole.

Their chosen modes of innovation—and innovation and experiment are most important to all—is in the long run conservative, anchored in convention, stereotype, and cliché. This odd marriage of convention and experiment assures that ambiguous relationship between form and substance in their works. Any one of the three might be accused of clinging to statement (in Ives's case, to the "program" of his music) at the expense of form—either to avoid formal judgment or to opt out of formal competition in the central artistic movements of his time. But we might just as readily charge any one of them with pursuing form at the expense of statement or substance, form for its own sake. Not only are both form and substance necessary for all three artists, but the integrated combination of form and substance is an article of their creeds. If we were to call Faulkner, Ford, or Ives a predominantly formal artist *or* a predominantly "message" artist, we should be wrong. But even in balance there is still in each a separation between form and substance. This might seem an anomaly. But each affinity—social, characteristic, formal, innovative—produces its own anomaly as readily as each characteristic adjectival description of the American produces its paired ambivalent adjectival epithet. Characteristic, personal, aesthetic, and formal anomaly and ambivalence seem to be the strongest threads common in their work.

For Faulkner, Ford, and Ives it took criticism some time to find out what was going on in the work: experiment was a barrier to understanding early in these careers. Before criticism could catch up, "sense of the canon"—criticism's intuition that the whole of the work made its own sense as Fordian, Ivesian, Faulknerian, independent of individual works—proved to be a godsend. "Message" or statement or substance was another anchor to the valuation of their work at its origins. Substance set forth broad outlines, a dominant consistency to latch on to. That everything Faulkner, Ford, and Ives did was consistent with most everything else they did was clear when little else was clear.

The sense of the canon is an arcane affinity and I have to argue it at some length. But if we begin at the opposite end, at the social affinity, perhaps we can find these artists and their common ground more accessible. Viewed simplistically, all three are late Romantic or turn-of-the-century men, men of an age of transition. This is more a personal tone or mood than it is an abstract ideal or a deliberate self-limitation. Their artistic ideals and aims are, indeed, so forward-looking that turn-of-the-century seems at first an absurdity. The experiment of Faulkner's fiction, Ford's movies, Ives's music contrasts strongly with the late Romantic tone or mood embodied in its creator's persona and pose.

Faulkner's and Ford's works have sometimes been grouped with post–World War I movements in American art, which would follow upon late Romantic persona and pose, but it is more logical stylistically to associate them with artists in America before that war, with Henry James and Edith Wharton, say, or Alfred Stieglitz, Frank Lloyd Wright, and Thomas Eakins, rather than with Gertrude Stein, Ernest Hemingway, or Alexander Calder (although of all these the strongest similarity is to Calder). Another way of stating their kinship with turn-of-the-century figures is by citing subject again: the work of all three turns inward toward America, rather than outward toward a European judgment or standard, and the "modern" in its definitive sense. All three were clearly more assimilative and inclusive than the expatriate generation could afford to be, perhaps because they knew better who they were.

This goes along with the next affinity: for Faulkner, Ford, and Ives the American Civil War is more significant than World War I. American literary history has been all too ready to divide its progress into phases designated by the nation's bellicosity; in this instance I think it makes a distinction clear. The patterns imposed upon America and Americans by the Civil War, best described by Edmund Wilson in *Patriotic Gore* (1964), find dynamic embodiment in the work of Faulkner, Ford, and Ives. The Civil War was *their* war as World War I was Hemingway's. Ford did more films of World War I and World War II than he did of the Civil War; *What Price Glory?* and *They Were Expendable* and the wartime documentaries spring most quickly to mind. But what I am arguing is not a locus of his sentiment or affections, and it is said even though none of the three had been of an age to come anywhere near serving in the Civil War. Faulkner served and Ford tried to serve in World War I, but the affinity for the Civil War remained in spite of Ford's World War I and II movies, Ives's *In Flanders Fields*, and the testimony of *Mosquitoes, Soldiers' Pay,* and Faulkner's many World War I stories.

These stories provide a case in point. This part of Faulkner's

fiction seems almost to have been written by another Faulkner, one trying very hard to measure up to the expatriate
alienation contemporary literary chic expected of him, one
kept very busy trying (somewhat as Joe Christmas mimics
Mame and Max in *Light in August*) to pick up the gestures and
movements of current fads and trends, but never quite manag-
ing to get it all straight. In *Sartoris*, John and Bayard's air war
(to say nothing of Young Bayard's deep-dyed between-the-wars
romanticism) never quite manages to dominate the omni-
presence of "The War"—the Civil War—and the shapes it
imposed upon the life of that novel. John Ford said the Civil
War was important to him because of two uncles (or four uncles) who had been in it, and declared himself a Civil War
buff. Anyone who sees *The Horse Soldiers* will find the declara-
tion superfluous.

But it is not just that these artists have an affinity for the
Civil War or espouse it before all other wars; it is that World
War I and its ideals do not provide an appropriate center
for them. To both Ford and Faulkner, the sardonic and self-
doubting romanticism characteristic of *Journey's End* or *A
Farewell to Arms* or *The Sun also Rises* is not just what is wanted
for the long haul of the career, and figures from a high romance, the Lost Cause, gallant gesture, Pickett's Charge, are
more apt.

Yet another function of that late Romantic personal image
should be mentioned here: Faulkner, Ford, and Ives all embrace the high Romantic self-image of the natural poet, the
pose of Walt Whitman. Perhaps more important, they prefer
this pose to the more international image of the cosmopolitan
man of the world, the aim of all good expatriate artists identified with World War I. For Raoul Walsh, for Ernest Hemingway, this pose was just the thing, but not for Ford or Faulkner.
None, of course, adopts Whitman's image without modifica-
tion. There is a bit of the dandy in Ford and Faulkner and (if
photographs are fit evidence) even in Ives. And sartorial manner finds a political base: none is a true Whitmanesque man of

the people, but like Oliver Wendell Holmes (as described by Edmund Wilson), each modifies his democratic pose and probably his democratic faith as well with protective elitist distance. They are all highborn democrats, hoping for some more elegant version of democracy than what they currently see at large. At the same time they know that some careful poses are now and again useful for keeping open connections to the common folk: Whitman's homespun shirt, funny hat, the oddly informal posture in the photo accompanying yet another version of *Leaves of Grass*; Faulkner's first *Time* cover photograph with the galluses; Ford's aircraft-carrier cap. In other words, each certainly sees something dangerous in Holmes's elitism and wants to set it off by Whitmanesque disguise.

Late Romantic sensibilities in highborn democrats are odd costuming, but even this is not all: one costume is not enough; they add disguise to disguise. Image, mask, disguise, impersonation, false face, artful dodging, take up an inordinate amount of their time. How silly all this looks thirty or forty or fifty years later and how one sometimes wishes that they might have shut up about who they were and gotten on with making what they could make. But we wish in vain, for these three are American artists, and who they want to seem to be is inextricably bound up with what they can make. This makes them sound devious. They are not. Image is so important to them, however, for a serviceable image is far harder to achieve than a simple political opinion is, and far harder to bring off consistently for a lifetime. The son of a town bandleader and the son of an Irish immigrant. Highborn? Well, yes. Sean Aloysius Feeney wanted the Naval Academy and took Hollywood. This is no proof. But bog Irish the Feeneys were not: there were not only aspirations but some small means, or the family could never have worked its way up the coast to Maine—perhaps helped by those uncles whose tales so fastened Ford upon the Civil War. Perhaps it was the sense an immigrant very soon develops that his aspiration is threatened by just the fact that he looks like the other immigrants, or that he doesn't want to stick around where there are a lot of them just like him. Maybe the Feeneys were upwardly mobile and sensed that Maine Irish might have an advantage over the New York Irish or Boston Irish. In any event, the disguise, the myth of origin Ford used in later life, was never poor immigrant or displaced person. Displaced gentleman, perhaps. His father kept a saloon, but you might be allowed to think he kept horses.

George Ives, that bandleader, got his son into Yale, perhaps partly by sending him to Hopkins Grammar School in New Haven: perhaps even the organ-playing jobs were part of a plan. We should not let our snobbish sense of what *bandmaster* means interfere here. It is an identity like any other, subject to individual and to cultural interpretation. Charles Ives quite seriously called his father "musician" and I think by this meant to distinguish one who cared about the aesthetic results and the system of music from one who merely worked regularly at music: he meant to put his father in the former category. *Bandmaster* still triggers one response, *musician* another, but that is our mind set, not Ives's. If George Ives had not had a little social status before he chose his vocation, Cousin Amelia Van Wyck would never have been able to look down so on his decision to become a bandmaster ("Of course Danbury thought that that was just kind of foolishness. Music and art were not things that you really worked at."[1]).

Highborn, in this instance, is a state of mind. They were highborn in their need to appear to be so, in that American need of, say, a Thomas Sutpen or a William Faulkner, posed rather incongruously in a bloom-colored coat mounted on his horse ready for the Oxford Hunt, or a John Ford, finally achieving in World War II that naval uniform and those commander's stripes, pausing to pose with Frank Capra for a photographer on the steps of some nameless church after some ceremony, or in front of some restaurant, confident that his navy uniform and the way he wears it go better with his pipe and aspirations than do Frank Capra's army uniform and cigarette. Dapperness is not the issue—in that, Capra (from the picture, at least) excels Ford—not the "dandy" of Stanley Cavell's categories,[2] but Ford's sense, apparent in the photo, that he is to the stripes and braid born, that he is the natural aristocracy, the Child of the Duke. See, for contrast, Capra's appeals to his immigrant background in his formal autobiography and in interview. Capra's myth of origin—not far removed from the Horatio Alger myth—contrasts to Ford's elaborate anecdotes of his mother and his brother Francis the putative highwayman, of himself and Francis taking on Hollywood as John Sartoris undertook the anchovy raid, confident that the gesture, the sallying forth—or derring-do—was more significant to his tall tales than whatever serious result that action might prove to have. Ford's anecdotes of his early life, like George Armstrong Custer's (or like V. K. Ratliff's), are tales of happy accident, of one man's stratagems, of cool manipulation, not of social rejection or economic struggle. For Faulkner it might be enough just to point out that he does not spare the Sartorises in his fiction *because* they were in some way patterned on the Falkners, but he does, ever so gradually, come to represent them in the fiction more and more as aristocracy proper (not earned or acquired), more proper than the Falkners or the Faulkners might legitimately claim to be.

Ives is a simpler case. In Ives's youth and for a good long time after, New Englanders claimed a national primacy that amounted to a kind of aristocracy by virtue of geography: then Brahmins still came from Boston and Concord glowed in a lingering sunset of mystique. Faulkner believes in this myth of the Northeast and acknowledges it in his descriptions of Joanna Burden's forebears in *Light in August* and of the Sutpen family's geographical slide in *Absalom, Absalom!*[3] The Yankees held firm title to claims the Southern aristocrat could but aspire to contend for, the title Westerners had, in part, come west to escape. Ford acknowledges this myth in *Drums Along the Mohawk*, in Doc Holliday's diploma (*My Darling Clementine*), in *Two Rode Together*, and tucked away in odd parts of his exploration of the new New World the West represented. New England is a past for all Ford's people, and its ghost rises when least expected.

These variant claims of region, subject to such ancient rules of primacy, bear upon this discussion because all these artists are regionalists. Ives claims the New England of Lexington and Concord as well as that of the Transcendentalists and that of the new industrial Northeast; Faulkner stakes out ante-bellum glories (and disappointments, as in "Was") together with Reconstruction and twentieth-century decay. Both come by their regions by heritage. Only Ford has to claim new ground as a settler might when he chooses the setting for his life's work. (Of course, his films of the South—*The Horse Soldiers, Judge Priest, The Sun Shines Bright*—and of Ireland have an importance of their own. I address here only that central threat of the West.) The Maine Irish buys into the West and finds the place which will make of him a first citizen, as it had of the Yankee farmer, the whore, the Eastern religious zealot, even, now and again, the Chinese immigrant or the Southern land-grabber—the only place which would favor the inter-loper over the holder of prior claims—claims prior (that is, short of) that ultimate prior claim of the Indian, of which Ford was always so conscious.[4]

The region so chosen does not go without saying. None is a "natural" place, the only place for Ives, Ford, or Faulkner to have settled down for a life's work. Ives might well have been expected to go the route of his contemporaries, to have chosen the more stylish identity of Henry James's Europe or the European conservatory; Faulkner, perhaps the transplanted alien's Europe; Ford could not perhaps have been expected to cleave completely to his Irish homeland for subject matter (in the manner of *The Informer, The Rising of the Moon, The Quiet Man*), but one might well have expected him to embrace that great creation of the Hollywood film, Murka as reinvented by the movies. That he chooses to reinvent and remake a partic-ular region in his films of family and in his Westerns instead

does not necessarily associate his work with what we now recognize as a great American genre, the Western. Those films
were not recognized as such when he got them going. It is,
rather, an act of dissociating himself from something he might
have aligned himself with if he had been more conventional,
from some latter-day "courtly muses," movies of the career
that pundits thought *The Informer* presaged for him: a brilliant
career of somewhat literary symbolic narratives.

But the courtly-muses explanation, as a matter of fact, fits
Faulkner and Ives as well. How mistaken it is to think that
Emerson's caution about the courtly muses of Europe was anchored in time: each generation has had to seek out new
courtly muses so as not to hearken to them. And each of these
artists knows his, and flees to regionalism in part to avoid them.
Ives avoids the Rollos and Nervous Nellies, the conservatory
ears of the too-comfortable public. Faulkner should never have
written *Sanctuary*, had he heeded one set of courtly muses, or
had he heeded another, he should never have gone on to do
the Trilogy. Fortunately he kept finding new courtly muses not
to hearken to.

To trace out the options available in these choices of region,
though, ignores a prior question: why do all three of these artists so depend upon assertive regionalism, preferring it to a
more accessible (indeed at the time practically endemic) nationalism? Nationalism is also important in their work, but
Faulkner, Ford, and Ives apparently had to get to nationalism
by progressing through regionalism. I think it's because they
aren't so much buying into anything as they are using whatever works for what they want to get done.

Regionalism had been a shape appropriate to the idea of
America in its beginnings and before the Civil War; it was the
mind set of the Founding Fathers and belonged to the debates
of *The Federalist*. The Civil War was a tragedy of region—regional interests acted as a splitting wedge to the Union and
nearly spelled an end to the possibility of nation. Regionalism
should have offended these artists as an idea whose time had

passed, an affront to their sense of themselves as up-to-date artists. But perhaps any purely external or historical reasons for picking or not picking a region do not address what's going on here. Ford's West, Ives's New England, Faulkner's South are too central to what the art embodies to be explained by historical compulsion or *Zeitgeist*: regionalism wasn't an idea running around at the time. Each could have selected this as a center for his life's work just *because* it was so old-fashioned—and so comfortable—so far off the beaten path of the cultural identity then in vogue and thus a stable basis for radical experiment and this interested each artist more than regionalism ever did anyhow. They could get to that experiment by working at first as regionalists.

Because all three are canon-builders—that is, makers of works which add up to a coherent whole—the choice of region is not lightly taken. The maker of such a canon, a composite epic in a sense, must pick his setting with great care because he picks for a lifetime.[5] This seems parochial but it isn't, because this regionalism is a way station on an orderly Platonic progression which leads to the national as surely as Object leads inexorably to Form. A number of other forms are found along this progress: regional shapes and forces become the mold for national characteristics and character; region can be metaphor or symbol for nation; or characteristic regional events or narratives can be taken together to make a national allegory. The South, the West, New England can by means of this progress be a little U.S.A.

Overt national feeling is always evident in these artists in the midst of their regionalism. In Faulkner's work, overt national feeling is seen in the stories of World War II ("Shall Not Perish," "Two Soldiers") the Trilogy, and some Indian stories ("Lo!"). There it is sometimes mistakenly taken to be embarrassing jingoism. It is really nothing much more than the way in which national interest or national concern contrasts to local or tribal or individual ignorance or shortsightedness. Nation is the larger picture, region the incomplete portion. Sometimes (as in "Two Soldiers") Faulkner's overt nationalism *is* irritating. But it's never there just to show the flag.

In Ives's heritage from his band-musician father—snatches of hymn, patriotic song, parlor song, and band tune—the memory of the songs' original "message" bears the burden of his overtly national substance. It is a mistake to think that Ives uses these songs with irony, but it is an equal mistake to think they are just popped into place so the piece will seem American. I think Ives uses them directly, as a part of his chosen identity.[6] He is a composer who uses borrowed tunes as motival units: this is his originality and his identity. Not only are they reminders of national identity and instant memories, but quotation of them—and the act of quotation itself—anchors Ives firmly in the heritage of Louis-Marie Gottschalk, Stephen Foster, Anthony Philip Heinrich, in American music's love of overtly American substance, embodied in historical and occasional program-music, in self-reference and self-allusion. It is no more jingoistic for Ives to employ such quotation than it is for Wordsworth to write sonnets. The way he uses them is unique, but that he feels compelled to use them welds him to the tradition.

Ford's overt Americanism is found in his tough and rather militant determination to show the flag, a determination that sometimes steams into his pictures with all the subtlety of the arrival of the Great White Fleet, accompanied by strummings of the *Red River Valley* or surges of *Battle Hymn of the Republic*. Again, jingoism is a misreading, a failure to see beyond the Stars and Stripes. This is instead another step in that Platonic progression: for these private and small-scale events there is also a higher measure beyond the local, the immediate, the regional, the appeal to a higher Form, to an unknown ideal approached only by passing through and beyond these things known. The American flag being raised over the stockade at the end of *Drums Along the Mohawk* is seen by the characters as unfamiliar. It will, Lana and Tom think, take some getting used to, but they like how it looks. A black woman we haven't noticed before in the movie looks up at the flag, Blue Back the friendly Indian gives it some sort of salute. Then they turn away, because they have to get on with the local business of living. This may be simple-minded or allegorical or even in some views silly or anticlimactic, but it is not jingoism.

Such appeals to regional and national allegiance seem, in part, to be moral matters. Each of these artists has a need to rediscover old-fashioned virtue. To do so they all choose what might seem to be nothing more than a nostalgia for simpler times. They have an affinity for the past. Faulkner's *The Reivers* is a nostalgic venture, but it is not nostalgic for nostalgia's sake. Rather it is nostalgia used and then devalued. *The Reivers* takes the narrator's nostalgia and through it makes whole a vision of a past unsullied by the complexity of our life now but still complicated by moral issues of "simple non-virtue." Nostalgia sets out to introduce us to a simpler world and is robbed of its softening light by the force of the issues raised in this supposedly "simpler" time.

Faulkner, Ford, and Ives use the past with seriousness and with a purpose. They strive in a variety of ways for a direct encounter with what is past: not just a casual reminiscence, a recapitulation, or a colorful rendering of it, but an examination and understanding of what it has to do with us, what we can gain or lose by it. They respect it and care about it—they don't simply yearn for it. All find something to admire in "old-fashioned virtue": the moral superiority they think was held by the generation just past. This is the subject matter for the early sections of Ford's *The Wings of Eagles* and some of *Steamboat 'Round the Bend*. It emerges in the turbulent courtship of *The Quiet Man*, the "togetherness" at the stockade in *Drums Along the Mohawk*, in the anchovy raid of *The Unvanquished*, some of Faulkner's Indian stories, some of the aspirations of Thomas Sutpen, most of the maunderings of Miss Rosa Coldfield (*Absalom, Absalom!*), Gavin Stevens's courtliness and many of his, V. K. Ratliff's, and Chick Mallison's failures to deal with the Snopeses (the Trilogy), much of the text of

Charles Ives's songs, the *Concord Sonata* (especially *The Alcotts*), and the music of his *Holidays* mood. None are just exercises in nostalgia. Ives's *Holidays*, for instance, is less a use of the past than an attempt to inhabit it.[7] Our regrets, our hopes of lessons to be learned from the past, comparisons between it and the time in which we find ourselves trapped, are all elements of this attempt, but it is more than a trip down memory lane or even, as a novelist I know says, stripmining it.[7a]

Ford, Ives, and Faulkner ask what it is proper or improper to make use of in the past, whether our use of it might have more to say about us now than about them then as we make our versions of the past in molds and forms of our own time. The excuse that these artists are late Romantics—that nostalgia is for them a comforting escape from a troubling present—is appealing but false. In nothing so much as their dynamic, unsentimental, direct uses of the past are Ives, Ford, and Faulkner distinctly and definitively twentieth-century men.

The way Ford handles the opening of *The Wings of Eagles*, as Spig Wead (John Wayne) crashes in the Admiral's pool, suggests this movie is to consist of sea story, the kind of yarn old salts exchange at the officers' club.[8] It has in its manner something of the personal feeling Ford obviously holds for Wead, who had worked with him on several pictures. One of the appeals such sea stories make upon the memory is precisely their failure to deal adequately or accurately with the past, their escape from the necessities of credibility or certitude or fact. Ford contrasts the training flight, the air-race adventures, the derring-do at the various officers' clubs of the movie with the domestic failure, the every-day drinking, injury, decay, and aging of Spig Wead. Later when Wead recalls the early events of the movie in the reduced images Ford gives us in those briefest of flashbacks, the director allows him to acknowledge the innocence of the self-delusion such roseate nostalgia represents. If *The Wings of Eagles* is nostalgia examined and judged for what it is, seen plain, it does not invite us to participate in delusion but asks us to understand what nostalgia is used for by these characters, to know its source, acknowledge its force, but not necessarily to adopt it as a practice ourselves. The rest of the movie proves that nostalgia is not an adequate handle on the past, and light-shot flashback images are not sufficient cause for the movie's dire effects: that can be found in the unexpected slip on the stair. Later in the movie Wead has laboriously recuperated from what seemed to be hopeless paraplegia. He then walks into the office of John Dodge (in real life, Ford's office) to talk about a job. When you walk into a stranger's office it is not your flying trophies or your sea-story past, not the practical jokes and boyish pranks of a career of derring-do, that determine where we end up in the real world. Flight training is this movie's anchovy raid, an ideal of simplicity for the movie's subsequent pain and suffering. But it proves a kind of fraud. The hero is not the man who can use the past that way.

In Faulkner's *The Unvanquished*, Granny tells tales of John Sartoris's dashing cavalry raid behind enemy lines just to get some anchovies for his supper, the quixotic gesture which for her embodies the reckless sense of honor of The War. Later she has become reduced from mistress of a plantation and her pretenses at aristocracy, to a common horse thief and mule trader, first for the Cause, but then for survival. She is finally murdered in the involutions of one of her deals. The principles or lack of principles in that original anchovy raid go unquestioned, but they are clearly negated in Granny's last horse trade. Raids and heroics, pennons flapping, are subject to harsher and even more damaging scrutiny in *Light in August*. The Reverend John Hightower is a spoilt minister—ruined in his town by a wayward wife, discharged by his church for the scandal and made a recluse, left on the sidelines by the community's rejection. More and more he finds his identity in the fantasies of his grandfather's wartime cavalry exploits during the War. He depends more and more on second-hand derring-do to call up false memories which aren't even his own. What nostalgia can do to the living is apparent in the tragic final fading glimpse of him "leaning forward in the window, his bandaged head huge and without depth upon the twin blobs of his hands upon the ledge, it seems to him that he still hears them: the wild bugles and the clashing sabres and the dying thunder of hooves."[9] Hightower finds first that the past haunts his days, then that it damns his present.

As I have said, Ives's use of old tunes is essentially straightforward, without irony, but this does not mean that such snatches are uninflected or simply recalled, remembered— whistled, as it were, in the midst of the pieces. They are used sometimes for their force and sometimes for their peculiar weakness, always to a purpose. Tunes and inversions or corruptions of tunes do not simply seek to profit upon that unearned (for Ives, at least) power inherent in the automatic allegiance a popular tune commands, but also are transformed into a new musical space, a new context for melodic exploration. Ives is conscious of the tunes as clichés, but he also carries with him a sense of what George Ives would have thought: that these old bits and pieces were sufficient in their own way, that they didn't need the reanimation or revitalization he could bring them by putting old wine in new bottles. So he recalls tunes that cast us back but finds in their sufficiency and in the new spaces his new use makes for them more force, more than the sum of such tunes themselves might add up to. With George Ives he loves the band and its parade; as Charles Ives he makes of their stuff a new space and then a new music.

Somewhere in these tunes, and somewhere in Faulkner's and Ford's familiar American substance as in their rather eccentric espousal of region, runs a common thread more significant than coincidence or parallel behavior. It is a yearning for center, a striving for middle. Walt Whitman, Frank Capra, John Steinbeck are all populist, or at any rate more populist than these three artists. This is not even yearning for popular success (as in Henry James and Sinclair Lewis). They are not seeking the average. Rather it is something which might be very crudely stated as a search for the heartland of art. Faulkner, Ford, and Ives all need a popular audience even though some of their disguises may obscure this. Disguise is less significant than is their need to become a part of the middle which America itself fancies itself to be and always seems to seek. Not so much Middle American (their ambivalent aspirations to Oliver Wendell Holmes elitism deny that) as it is centrist, a seeking of the midst. So much of what Ford shows us on the screen appeals to this centrism that many critics have mistaken him for a populist, assuming his films to provide a comfortable, coherent narrative of Middle American aspirations. So what if his films may indeed stray now and again into happy myth, the main idea is still no more than good America, America plain. Peter Bogdanovich uses something not much more complex than this fake populism for the thesis of his anthology film, *Directed by John Ford*. To see only this is to ignore not only the darkness of his films—not just limited to *Two Rode Together*, *The Searchers*, *Liberty Valance*, but the dark side always present even in Ford's happiest films—but to miss the point of his centrism. Ford concentrates on the community, but this is not to say he feels the community is always right or even that the community is a happy league of contented individuals. Ford is as interested in tension between community and individual as Faulkner is, and his films perhaps even go beyond this: Ford takes community as his subject. Centrism is a part of that tension: the cost to individuals of banding into communities, the cost to community when it stifles individuals. *Stagecoach* offers a stunning example; the same kind of comment can be found in the cultural rule of law in *The Hurricane*. The group which has set out on the journey to Lordsburg is a microcosm of individual lives, developments, isolations, joinings, and this little world produces a constantly shifting norm of duty, ethics, behavior, justice. The people (in *The Hurricane*, community unspecified as individuals surround Terangi's escape) provide the center; the situation provides the test which the individuals cannot solve without moment-to-moment guidance from the center that community provides. When the stagecoach gets to its destination, the group then has to work out its individual ideals in the context of the town (Ringo to his shootout, the whore to the town's scorn, the embezzler to his arrest).

The attribution of centrism to Ives may seem willfully wrongheaded, for he so frequently and deliberately seems to line up with the opposition, with the obscurantist or eccentric. Ives's obscurantism is not so much a principle of his art as it is the motto of his behavior. He has a need not to be known, a need to fade into the woodwork, and the ambivalent pairing for this is a need to join the steeples and mountains and countryside as another feature of the landscape. This constant tug-of-war between being known and fading away, centric and eccentric, is more significant than some tic of personal style. It has a great deal to do with the balance between gratification of audience at hand and innovative experiment, between pleasing us and pleasing himself. Such a balance is at the center of the work of all three of these American originals.

Probably Ives's dislike of being photographed and getting his name in the papers, Ford's built-in regret that an interview is taking place, Faulkner's diffidence at meeting the public, are all parts of the same aversion, and the segregation of art from commerce in Ives's case, the cover story of "making pictures" for Ford and of "boiling a pot" for Faulkner, perhaps tied up with the struggle each had with his father about identity.

Psychoanalytic depth is not an aim of this study, but perhaps one instance would lend perspective here. George Ives was faced not just with the problem of making bandmastering respectable, but also with the consequent cost to his family. Charles Ives's choice of the insurance business as locus for his energies and professional attentions was probably sparked, somewhere in its deeper drives and sources, by a need to recompense some of his father's costs to his family (or at least not to force *his* family similarly to underwrite his art). Ives is a complex sum. The story his career tells can be stated in many different ways, all absolutely American but each a distinctly different myth: (1) Here was a true amateur musician, but a genius (even if we call it a hobby we cannot denigrate the product). (2) Ives was a musician, yes—a musical dabbler—but never an artist. (3) Ives the musical genius was using the insurance business as a front to help him avoid the terrible costs and compromises any self-proclaimed artist must face in America. (4) The candle under the bushel is also in the American grain—Edward Taylor, Emily Dickinson, Herman Melville—and Ives was the supreme example of the isolation of that hard, gemlike flame of genius under the bushel of the insurance game. (5) The insurance game provided money and a power base essential to bring Ives's music to the attention of the people who eventually would see to it that it would be heard: the whole career was carefully calculated *to appear to be* obscure genius, but was instead the product of a commuting advertiser's commercial genius.[10] Or, finally, (6) Ives, suspecting he could not make it as an artist, and fighting shy of the example of his father's compromise, sold out but in the end came out smelling like a rose because our fashion in genius shifted at just the right time for his kind of genius suddenly to seem the very thing.

Every telling is ambivalent: one side of each assertion tends to undercut the other side of the next. There is the probability that Ives (in whichever version, or in all six) was involved in some kind of pose, mask, or disguise.

I have already suggested the pose and disguise manifest in two Faulkners: the gallus-snapping, down-home, cracker-barrel, just-folks Bill; and the man of letters with the black passport in the Cartier-Bresson photos at West Point.[11] Ford is a tougher case, but the image projected in Ward Bond's "John Dodge" the director character of *The Wings of Eagles*, even though fictional, must somehow be brought into alignment with the laconic interviewee Bogdanovich interrogates in his *Directed by John Ford*, a man of impatient and monosyllabic replies to what he obviously feels are stupid questions.

This issue and the attendant issue of the tension between

centric and eccentric, lie at the heart of America's treatment of anyone American who announces an intention to be seen as an artist. In order to presume to be an American artist, one needs to be (like Donny and Marie Osmond—a little bit country and a little bit rock-and-roll) a little bit Whitman, but in order to show us he has made it, that he has finally arrived, he must deny even that little bit because, after all, he is an American and would not think of paying to have his books published. He must, in other words, become respectable, be the man of letters along the European lines the Establishment prefers. What I single out is not the need of a genius to be a moneymaker—which is, after all, beside the point for most of Faulkner's career and all of Ives's, and went with the territory for Ford's—but a need to satisfy the American urge to look successful, or, more important, America's need for its artists to look successful. Starving we do not like. We want our geniuses to wash up, but once they have, O quandary, O paradox, we can no longer be sure they are our geniuses. Once any one of them declares he is an artist, he recognizes the ground rules have changed, and so do we. Ives is of two minds about competing in this ball game at all, much less about appearing to compete. He's not sure he even wants to put on the uniform.

A misconception of centrist art might lead us to expect a tendency toward the kind of heroes populism advances, or at least the literary heroism of protagonism (something like: we must be up and doing, for we are in a book), a significant action organized around the individual. Heroes and heroism are not, after all, far from the late Romantic personal pose. Yet another possible reading of Ives's career could see him casting himself as a hero of music, taking the stance of the deliberately obscure genius or the pose of that Titan he thought his times demanded, Titan as antihero. Ives searches for an American hero, or antihero, depending on how one reads the piece (in *Concord Sonata* and in some of the more programmatic music; heroics are frequently found in the texts of *114 Songs*).

The antihero looms so large in Faulkner's fiction that it is perhaps difficult to find there any deep attraction toward hero at all. Even to seek the antihero of course is to seek a protagonist.

In Ford the conventional meaning of hero is drastically re-defined as his work advances (or sometimes—as in *Two Rode Together*—in the course of a single film). It is difficult to be-lieve that the man who formed his late antiheroes could have made the early heroes and could have believed in them as firmly as it seemed he did, or as firmly as he makes us believe in them every time they flash on the screen. But in Ford the mixture of hero and antihero is less apparent both early and late than his constant all-too-human protagonist. Centrism is not consistent rhetorically in terms of heroes. But in these three artists heroics and antiheroics, centrist ends are being sought by artists who in their personal poses are eccentrics. Another set of masks, some further personal ambivalence.

The most important product of centrism is canon—the in-tegrity and unity of total output, of career, of *opera*—and this only makes more anomalous the relationship found in these three originals between centric and eccentric. That the canon is a significant critical and analytical unit, that the artist's consciousness of it affects his sense of what he is doing, that it interacts with his formal sense of each individual work, is proved nowhere more easily than with these three artists.

Sense of the canon for Ford, Faulkner, and Ives was a lively concern and a factor significant historically to the criticism of their works. Sense of the canon is a critic's model which does not necessarily depend on the artist's intention to form a canon or on his knowledge or realization that what he has done has begun to look like a canon. Just as clearly it is a model whose appeal and convenience ought to make one wary of its legitimacy. None of these three artists sets out to con-struct just exactly the canon he ends up with, even though it is clear that each at every stage thinks he will end up with a considerable body of work, and none seems to question that when he's finished the parts will look like each other. Indeed none seems ever to have questioned that he could keep on going until he ran out of life to go on with, and only one (maybe because of illness) ran out before he was dead—and even he may just have stopped.

Canon is everything an artist has done which can be read together as a whole when he has finished. Canon does not impose the necessities of any smaller formal sequence, such as trilogy or tetralogy, or even those of a movie serial or a song cycle: it does not know certainly when it is ending any more than it knows when it begins; it does not develop in the formal manner a single filmic, literary, or musical structure might take. An artist does not know when his canon has begun to take on a shape or a "sense," when it has reached its high point; sometimes he does not even know it is there at all, or know everything his canon involves (any more than he would necessarily know everything which emerges from his work) in its connections, work to work. In many ways canon is less a structure in any of the conventional formal senses than a biological organism is a structure. A biological or biochemical model may be appropriate for canon because it stresses a single shape clear to every artist and universally acknowledged—any organic system strives, as the canon does, for survival. This need to survive becomes a necessary shaping force that overcomes (in both models) all other drives, aims, shapes, and ends.

Canon is complex. Its impact can be unified and profound, its effect easy to comprehend and distinguish, and its usefulness perfectly apparent. In some artists, such as Ford, Ives, and Faulkner, its significance is paramount. To perceive the shape of canon in their work is more than a matter of critical convenience: it is an essential to understanding. A crucial unity of their work rests on knowing that the parts contribute to the whole in a canonical way.

This could be said perhaps of any artist's *opera*: we read Keats for the poems, but the letters serve our reading of the poems. I mean canon as a stricter structure than *opera*. Knowing one piece in the artistic work of one of these artists serves the knowing or penetration or understanding of the next and of any other of his individual works: that is canon. What stretches from work to work is more than just style or common subject: what is Fordian or Faulknerian or Ivesian about a particular piece matters more to both that piece and to the canon than the stylistics of a piece by Prokofiev or Verdi. Even *style* in the sense musicians give to that word does not cover canon: the characteristic excesses, the essential hallmarks of the norm, our understanding of the center of particular works, coextensive space, shared shapes and volumes, coordinate time systems, are a part of canon.

Sometimes it is simplistic to begin the examination of an artist by exaggerating or stretching the artist's extremes or gaucheries—even to parody the work by stressing their excesses or self-parodies. With Faulkner, Ford, and Ives the excesses are a part of canonical identity, a part of the mature critical understanding of the experience of viewer/reader/hearer as well as that of the beginner. They need not be stretched or exaggerated because that stretching is part of the whole. It is some measure of maturity in the viewer/reader/hearer that he can consent to work with such apparent clichés. With few other artists are both the unique line of the individual work so closely supported by the canon of the work in general, and the more general excess, aberration, manner, or norm, so central to what these artists are doing in each individual work, so close to the center of what they are about.[12]

The innovation of an individual work may well differentiate it from the rest of the canon, or perhaps make clear a development it represents beyond what happened in the canon before it came along. It may be part of a progression of successive works (as in Ford's cavalry trilogy, or Faulkner's Snopes Trilogy). At the same time innovations set a pattern of expectation for what is to come. It is difficult to associate a particular innovation with any single work especially in the work of such complex artists as Faulkner, Ford, and Ives. But there seems always to be an interdependence between the familiar—convention, cliché—and the unfamiliar—radical, innovative, outrageous, startling. What is familiar acts as anchor for our attentions and sensibilities so that the unfamiliar can be slipped in—familiar pre-domesticates the unfamiliar for us.

In Ford's *The Hurricane* we watch a South Seas picture, sarongs and all.[13] Or (more appropriate to today's genres) we see a disaster picture, beautifully photographed with stunningly spectacular special effects. Ford encloses in it Terangi's escape, an action narrative which is the sum of all generic escape attempts and their highest measure at the same time—an abstraction of a simple set of actions to their essentials.

Faulkner in *As I Lay Dying* uses substance not far removed from Erskine Caldwell's hillbilly local color, bad dirty songs, or Ozarks joke-books, and makes of this material a tragic abstraction of individual and interactive fates, an experiment in the consciousness of multiple voices as complex as any in fiction, set down in substance similar to an *Esquire* hillbilly cartoon of the Thirties. Ives in *America Variations* takes the tune of *My Country 'Tis of Thee* as motif for an innovative set of formal variations—and then explores the nature of what variants do to their original, makes the variations into a sequence almost more programmatic than formal. A Whitman disguise makes the Wendell Holmes aristocratic stance more acceptable; familiar domesticates experimental; American substance familiarizes aesthetic innovation.

Something like this familiar/unfamiliar relationship might be said to exist between the characteristic shape in a particular work and the general characteristic norms of the canon we are already familiar with from other works. Here too the familiar predisposes us to the unfamiliar. But more than that: having become unaccustomedly used to surprise by innovation, we await innovation with a conditioned expectation that we *will* be surprised. We come to respond to an innovation not with a jump or a jerk, not as we might to a disruption, but rather with a smile of recognition and expectation. We are in on the game and can figure this one out, too. We have been here before and now return in part at least because we prefer the smile of recognition to the jolt. It's also more of an insider's game.

This is rudimentary: it overexplicates a shape which has almost become a cliché of criticism: initiation, the pride an initiate feels when he finds that he has fathomed the mysteries, the delight of the shaman in lording it over the innocents once again. But something like this rudimentary understanding of initiation is the sense of the canon I am trying to argue—an experience circular in its surprises, repetitive, its aberration become almost norm-setting. If we refuse to move to the canon's rhythms of expectation and gratification, we do not deal fully with Faulkner, Ford, or Ives. Because—and this is most important—the canon is this far at least a conscious part of the art.

Come, says Faulkner, see if you can master the way Benjy Compson's mind associates one thing with another as he watches the golfers (in the opening of *The Sound and the Fury*). Then if I make it all simpler and simpler for the rest of the novel you may wonder where the true complexity lies—in hard words or in simpler meanings. But having done that you may well become suspicious every time you come to a sudden jump in time, sensitized so that a nonsequential section of *As I Lay Dying*—Vardaman's "My mother is a fish," for instance—sets off a complex chain reaction in you. Come, says Ives, sit still for my *Shall We Gather at the River?*, a familiar hymn sung to a slightly but profoundly different tune; those wrong notes and the right ones you go on hearing in spite of my tune may soon make you ready for notes you cannot hear but are there nonetheless in the *Third Symphony*, then for shadow-notes, then for melodies you supply at the end of songs when I have started but do not finish the National Anthem. Come, says

Ford, see the attraction of the Marshal (Henry Fonda) who totes no gun and balances himself on the porch post, left foot, right foot; then you will be ready for *Two Rode Together*'s Guthrie McCabe (James Stewart) who does the same and looks the same in every regard but who is a corrupted contradiction to *Clementine*'s Wyatt Earp. The second undercuts everything the first bears as honest, yet the manner, the appeal, the down-home come-on is just the same. And it reads backward—Earp to McCabe—as clearly as it reads forward chronologically. For this is canon and its order is its own. What is here now can mean what has been as well as what will be.

All this might be characterized as a function of style or an imprint of personal manner. I think it is more. With Faulkner the canon's continuities involve such things as survival of characters from book to book (V. K. Ratliff, Quentin Compson, Mink Snopes), thematic continuity through several novels (ownership, incest, heritage), and extension of habitual modes of narrative (omission suspense, stop-action, depiction of violent movement, rendition of consciousness, dramatic exchange). This is not just style and in some instances not at all personal. Such continuities of canon invite us, seduce us, coax us along, dare us as reader, as viewer, as hearer, to risk a bit and come along, to see it through one more work. Calls upon the initiate are more complex in their multiple appeals than that cliché of initiation implies.

This suggests that canon connections between one work and the next are characteristic. They are also dynamic: the biological model is again appropriate. The elements in the work that link or unify it to the canon are not just customary or characteristic ingredients but essential foundations for the experiments the artists devise upon them. Faulkner, Ford, and Ives demanded canon: Ives writes not only variations (this could be formal or stylistic) but adds repetition and variation of motif, stretchings and squeezings of notation. His continual experiment at the edge of our sense of score approaches score itself as experiment: what score can or cannot do to approach the sound Ives has heard in his head and expects us to hear as well. With Ford, continuities include repetition and continuation of stock characters, a continuing company of actors, a repeated natural setting (Monument Valley in particular), repeated tunes in the score, and changing manifestations of any of these as formal, symbolic, and abstracting devices. All this and a growing repertory of repetition in the poetry of gesture, of ritual, movement, and myth.

With few other artists does canon loom so large: it is almost impossible—or at least seems perverse—to think about *Light in August* or the *Concord Sonata* or *The Searchers* without calling to mind *Go Down, Moses*, or the *Three-Page Sonata* or *Three Godfathers*. The examples multiply. Without being joined to the rest of the canons of which they are a part, the canons which in a sense form their settings, these magnificent works are like severed heads, lacking the rest of themselves. Certainly individual works can be thought of alone. Their formal integrity and independence is as good as the next work's—this is not what I mean. But why should I so need to bring V. K. Ratliff and Ike McCaslin to bear on a discussion of Byron Bunch? to discuss Colonel John Marlowe of *The Horse Soldiers* together with John Wayne's other role as Ethan Edwards in *The Searchers*? to parallel Ives's song and symphony when the formal differentiation between the two would in another artist make such comparison absurd? It is because the sentence "Because that's what Ford/Ives/Faulkner does" can become as comfortable a reference for me as critic as "Because I said so" can for me as an arbitrary parent. As comfortable, but I would argue, more justified. To know the experiment of *Sanctuary* serves the understanding of the very different experiments of *Light in August*, to know how Ives uses juxtaposition of musical ideas in a song like *The Side-Show* (No. 32) serves the analysis of his structure in the *Third Symphony*, to understand the strange opening of *Wagon Master* as Uncle Shiloh kills a man in cold blood, is to begin work on the ending of *Two Rode Together* and its sudden lynching.

Canon as I use the word here includes the total product of the artist, his *opera*. I don't want to suggest that all the parts and pieces are as significant to an artist's canon as some are. The most useful definition of canon is the total coherent product, works which taken together establish a coherence which can enhance the force of the works considered one at a time. It would make no sense to exclude *The Wild Palms* from Faulkner's central canon, but it might be appropriate to set aside *Knight's Gambit* even though its central character is far more significant to the mainstream of Faulkner's fiction than any of the characters in *The Wild Palms*. The Old Man half of *The Wild Palms'* double narrative is a Yoknapatawpha story, and parallel in some ways to *As I Lay Dying* and the wandering and death of Mink Snopes in the Trilogy. Detective stories, even detective stories with Gavin Stevens as the detective, aren't in the same ball park. The decision rests on relevance to the fiction's—the canon's—central force. All of Faulkner's short stories seem to me to belong more to the sense of the canon, seem more to partake of its continuing norms and tendencies, than do any of the poems and more, even, than *Knight's Gambit* or *Mosquitoes*. Some of John Ford's silent features seem appropriately grouped in the canon of the main body of his work in sound film, but if one were to attempt to include all of them and devote critical attention of the same sort to *Little Miss Smiles* as to *My Darling Clementine*, it would be not only exhausting and arcane but silly. *Clementine* is at the center of his Westerns, and much of what prepares us to watch a Ford, much of that *familiar* so essential to the interaction of innovation with what is down-home, didn't really get started in Ford's work until the mid-Thirties. The silents cannot be looked at in this way (as is true of so many silent canons today), because what survives is spotty—and because for most canons there is a great gulf fixed between style, narrative, image, performance, genre—of silent and sound films.

The point is a subtle one. If a critic were dealing with Wordsworth instead of with Faulkner, it might be obvious that he would legitimately dismiss much of the later work as not very interesting, as well as some of the very early and certain parts of the early and middle work. This is done not just in survey courses in colleges, but in detailed critical studies of Wordsworth. If the limitations of space were acute a critic might select poems to discuss according to significance or "weight"—to discuss "Ode: Intimations of Immortality" and "Elegiac Stanzas" rather than "We Are Seven" and "Resolution and Independence." The same would be true of Faulkner: *Light in August* would be more significant to discussion than *Sartoris* would. But this is not what I'm trying to make of canon.

These canons—Ford's, Ives's, Faulkner's—are different in kind from others in the same arts contemporary to them. *Sartoris* better serves the understanding of *Light in August*, *Some Southpaw Pitching* serves better the understanding of *The Second Symphony*, *The Wings of Eagles* is more applicable to any other title in Ford's canon and the shape of the canon as a whole than is "Michael" to the *Prelude*, Eliot's "Sweeney Agonistes" to *The Waste Land*, Schoenberg's *Moses and Aaron* to the *4th Quartet*, or Von Sternberg's *Morocco* to *Blond Venus*.

Style is included in canon, but style is by no means all that is at issue. Return to that sense of an organic structure: canon is not just a network of overlapping similarities or parallels, work to work, or continuing themes, extension of characters, but the continuance of our involvement in Ives's music throughout his music, from one work to the next, our sense of the formal relationship between Ford's films and the continuation of our relationship to *My Darling Clementine* in *Cheyenne Autumn*, the continuity between new work and old (*Seven Women* and *Stagecoach*; "A Rose for Emily," "Was") from old to new, from recent (*Fourth Symphony*) retraced to early (*Slow March*). The relationship between artist and work, our achieved and considered critical sense of how he approaches this work, how he proceeds with it, what he thinks he is constructing, and what matters to him, go to make up a sense of his canon. Relationships, not common characteristics, are the centerline of the study of canon. The whole is an organism, not a chart.

Faulkner's fascination with the spaces and distances involved in the shift from subjectivity to objectivity, the gulf he fixes between intense imprisonment in a single consciousness in *The Sound and the Fury* (both his imprisonment as artist and ours as readers) and the more relaxed freedom of omniscient but still subjective narration in *Light in August*, the distance between the Bundrens as they see themselves in *As I Lay Dying* and the Bundrens as they are seen by Armstid, Peabody, and MacGowan from outside the family, informs a much later and more subtle experiment. In *The Town* we see the narrators now burdened by this dual role as tellers of and synchronous participants in the story. The costs and rewards of subjectivity are a constant theme in Faulkner, but to state this accomplishes little compared to the detailed tracing of subjective and objective spaces as they occur work to work.

The Town's narration refers backward to *Absalom, Absalom!* There the truest tale of Thomas Sutpen is concocted, devised, invented, and polished at the greatest possible distance from the actions and facts of Thomas Sutpen, in a frozen Harvard Yard years after his death. *Absalom, Absalom!* in its turn looks to an otherwise unmemorable short story, "Artist at Home," in which the narrator canot resist revising the actions he is about to take in order to improve the story he is in the process of writing about them. The time disjunctions of the first section of *The Sound and the Fury* are a rehearsal for the way the narrative presence manipulates us to a different measure in *Light in August*; the constants of fire and Caddy's smell like trees in the earlier novel find an echo in the later book in our continual return to home base, the column of smoke from the Joanna Burden place. Abstract predeterminations and causalities seen in Quentin's intellectualized fatalism are made more concrete and credible in the predestinations and causalities of Joe Christmas's internal clock, the tickings of his private infernal machine.

Ford's imprisonment and escape sequence in *Prisoner of Shark Island* is repeated in *The Hurricane* with the same jailer (John Carradine) and a very different escapee (spirit turned animal rather than, in the former, intellect turned animal). It is reanalyzed, takes a different part in the work which surrounds it, moves us in a different, more detailed, more emotionally involving way. The hospital sequence in *The Wings of Eagles* is another version of that escape sequence, as Spig Wead (John Wayne) is challenged to force himself to walk. The jailer has become the prodding, ukulele-strumming chief-petty-officer buddy (Dan Dailey) and the challenge to escape is now mirrored in the formal restriction of our angles, our imprisonment of concentration in the gurney which traps Wayne and quite literally in his mirror by which his world is measured, a tiny reflection which gives him his only vantage. Some elements of that sequence recur in a very different context in *Two Rode Together*, as McCabe returns to the whites in the wagon-train settlement the white captive boy turned Indian. We are given the zoo's eye view of that imprisonment in a cage, the escape sequence repeated now with its rhetorical guides removed, the escape of a savage in spite of himself by his murder of a lady crazy in spite of herself who thinks she's his mother, which will motivate his fully willed and fully conscious lynching by his own people who had fetched him back in the first place.

I have already invoked the Whitman pose as man-of-the-people disguise, as the barbaric yawp of the proper American artist, as antidote to the cosmopolitan man of letters in the European mold, defense against whatever courtly muses should happen to eventuate. I shall invoke it just once more as a Whitman left hand which experiments, innovates, tries things in a new, shocking, more revolutionary way, while the right hand, our Washington Irving perhaps, sits back and oversees what has been done, tidies it up, conventionalizes and traditionalizes the whole so that none of that left-handed work will seem out of place or unexpected, surprising, or awkward. In this model, strangely, it is the southpaw Whitman who, as Faulkner would say, "pleases himself," and Irving who is intent on pleasing the house, charming the audience, coaxing the crowd into the tent, and keeping it there so that the bumptious Whitman can go into his act.

Experiment in art can be in several kinds. One is the pursuit of a manner known as "the experimental," recognized by audience and critic alike as having been aimed at the world of artistic experiment from the start, emerging from its experimental tradition. Such experiment is careful to opt out of the mainstream, to delimit its appeal to those who can recognize the values of avant-garde limitations of audience, accessibility, or engagement. John Cage and the late Gertrude Stein offer this kind of "experimental" work to a predetermined, and pre-narrowed audience for "the experimental." Part of the point of doing avant-garde work is not that it will offend general audiences: it is not offered to them, but only to an audience from which the general has been carefully omitted. When a wandering member of the general audience happens into a play by Robert Wilson, discovers it's boring (to him), and leaves, he is liable to be cheered or jeered by the self-selected prelimited audience. The artist seeks the initiated, smaller (and sometimes minuscule) audience for it. This sort of experiment appealed to Faulkner only very early (some sketches, some poems, some short stories), to Ford and Ives probably never.

Experiment can also be on the order of a popular idea of scientific experiment: this is a crazy idea but it just might work, a trial-and-error fooling-around with form, technique, voice, structure, and sequence. The experiment of Faulkner, Ford, and Ives was almost never pursued in this form; rather it is somewhere between I'll-do-it-this-way-till-it-comes-right and a more staid experiment, clearly identified for the artist only after the fact. Before the fact they sometimes don't know it is experimental; they may even have thought it was going to turn out to be an ordinary story.

All three of these artists want an audience, but want a work that will stretch the audience. If the work is unconventional in its appeal, so much the better. The artist needs to know it has "worked" before he releases it, but he has no qualms about releasing a rather intimidating piece as long as he himself is sure it *has* worked: the experiment, in other words, may have started out as an experiment in the unknown, but it has turned into an innovation in the now-known. Experiments that fail do not ordinarily reach the screen, the printed page, or the finished score. But I think that Faulkner viewed A *Fable* as an experiment that worked, that Ford thought *The Fugitive* was working, or would work when released and only later became disillusioned with it when everybody (including the folks at the box offices) said it was a failure, and then, as his statements imply, became foolishly fond of it.[15] I doubt that much of Ives's "unplayable" music—that which really is unplayable and is not just another instance of the stretching and bending of notational modes or of current inability to figure out some way to play it—was clearly an experiment that did not work; or was an experiment that would have to be categorized in some manner more akin to "the experimental," something with a predetermined experimental or theoretical nature, its audience preshrunk to music theorists.

To discuss the innovation or experiment of any of these three in a way general to all is almost impossible: the innovations in fiction introduced by Faulkner probably outnumber those used first by any other artist with the possible exception of Proust or Joyce, or, I suppose, Richardson; Ford, those of anyone save D. W. Griffith. This kind of measure of innovation is more or less meaningless for anything besides some kind of *Guinness Book of World Records* chart: what is wanted instead is some sense of what innovation or experiment is aimed at, whether general tendencies of experiment can be isolated, the distance between the experiment as it might be viewed by the common reader/viewer/hearer and as it might be viewed by the critic.

Charles Ives was surely determined to change the listener's idea of what proper music is. "Proper" was a category which meant a great deal to him and which meant he felt, the wrong thing to most of his listeners. To him it meant something worth listening to, music trying to do something. To his listeners he felt it meant a kind of garden club, or kind of appropriateness or palatability, a don't-rock-the-boat propriety he determined, very early on, to alter. Innovation in the first instance meant to him an exploration of some issues of "Why not this way instead of that?" or "Can you now listen to this instead of that?" or "Can you, now that you've tried that, manage this?" Innovation was a means to an end—the end being a liberated sort of music for a liberated ear, a new freedom from some of the bondages of habit and tradition and the wrong arbiters of taste ruling the concert hall, Rollos and Nervous Nellies. Not really a new beginning for all of music as Wordsworth claimed for all of poetry, Ives's own myth of experiment was more humble, or, since humble seems so odd a choice of word for Ives, more realistic in its estimate of one man's power to change so entrenched a system as music was when he found it.

For Ford innovation was also a means to an end, but the end was so sharply different from that of Ives as to be almost unidentifiable with it. Ford did not particularly want to "show them," in the sense of reforming the taste of America or its arbiters. He did want to stretch the limits of what the screen had been accustomed to offer, but not so much to turn it away from traditional or accustomed values as to make it over as a more subtle, more sensitive, more feeling instrument. His work managed to identify the Western as a respectable genre, a centerpiece of American film *because* his experiments so sensitized the rather intractable format he found. He found in the Western an arrangement of manipulable clichés and stereotypes; he manipulated this unpromising material and invented new material—new subjects, new stock characters, until the

Western became a responsible language of human action; with this language he made the most flexible generic instrument in American art. He found, recognized, and made anew signs and symbols—but more important, he constructed in his films a new vision, a way to see human behavior freed of the cant that so often attends old tales. He integrated these traditional patterns with forms from his non-Western films—of family (the small town becomes the settlement), of the military (the Foreign Legion becomes the U.S. Cavalry), of solitude and community. He honed and reformed the habitual devices of American framing, editing, and rhythm into a new instrument of virtually musical expressiveness and complexity, so that the force of his grand sweep is matched with an almost microscopic perfection of detail in human gesture.

All of this development and refinement of form make possible a stunning force of subject matter. He makes a full canon of American individual and community character against this reinvented landscape. In the early and middle period he explores some values and in the later years he questions, probes, doubts those values to find a more "realistic," less optimistic or, in other terms, less opportunistic vision of the American and of the individual put to a bizarre test. This is something less than a denial of all he formerly held dear, and to say he turns bitter in old age is simply wide of the mark. By the end of his career he has made something far more profound than the American film up until then has been capable of. It is as if Faulkner's early violence, his disjunctive, bizarre, sometimes gothic, nay-saying occurred to Ford late, with Faulkner's later mellowness of theme and structure and conclusion coming much earlier. Of course this also makes possible a handsome mix Faulkner could not have: the discretion of age and the finesse of means applied to the dark side.

Ford's experiment also (and here experiment is difficult to separate from experience) brought him a visual style which, like Jean Renoir's ultimately defies formal analysis because it defies anatomy or analysis by chart or sequencing. This is just why both artists so demand intense and detailed visual analysis. Orson Welles wore out his print of *Stagecoach* with good reason, for the visual abstractions alone give us pause just to think of them, to run the film through our heads: the drunken doctor (Thomas Mitchell) seen against the geometric pattern of the light reflections on the bar in the way station, the stagecoach crossing the almost palpable border between dark desert and white. We can lay out in sequence what happens in the lightning-swift lynching near the end of *Two Rode Together*; some of the timing and the musical turns of the climax of that film are possible to analyze schematically, but no shot-by-shot analysis can include the rhythmic satisfactions, empathetic gratifications, and formal perfections of these sequences as they are viewed in context, and as the films of which they are small parts are viewed as a whole or as a part of Ford's canon. Like Renoir's *melée* at the house party's amateur theatricals in *The Rules of the Game*, such invention, innovation, experiment anticipate visual needs we did not have the wit to know we had, gratify those needs and then go beyond them to something new.[16]

Faulkner's experiment was, in a way, more personal than that of Ives or Ford. In it he sought an escape from the curse which fell on major American writers (save Henry James), that break which seems always to interrupt the continuous arc which otherwise rounds out a completed career.[17] The disappointment inherent in the change in late Emerson essays, Melville after the breakdown—in, for instance *The Confidence Man*—Hawthorne after *The House of the Seven Gables*, are clearly working a path different from the one they started out on. Faulkner sought a way to free himself of the kind of age debilitation, failure of nerve, breakdown that struck his fellow American writers. The experiments serving Faulkner's personal search for narrative freedom were perhaps even more significantly sequential and developmental than those of Ford. In the novels of consciousness (*The Sound and the Fury*, *As I Lay Dying*, for instance) Faulkner sought ways to render with ease the inner voices of an individual, an aim he shared with many moderns, but he gave time and memory a far more significant role in forming both character and response, and thus in shaping action in the latter (in *Absalom, Absalom!*, *Light in August*). Individual decisions made within imprisoned consciousnesses are subject to the accidental invasion from the outside world and from within by less-than-conscious habit and tic and less-than-verbal cues for passion buried deep in the past and even deeper in the consciousness. In his later experiments Faulkner built upon this as he related consciousness to the simpler matters of oral tradition (*Absalom, Absalom!*), linked tale-spinning to modern developments of time, memory, and consciousness (the Trilogy). His experiments both early and late led to an extremely rich texture which retained the original alienation of the early novels but later dealt as well with less conventional matters of community, morality, problems of coerced, inborn, and chosen roles. What developed from all this was an epic, a leviathan anatomy of age, of sex, of class, and of love. The experiments in hindsight seem less chancy than they were because now the results are so clear.

All these affinities and experiments lead to parallelism between these three artists that is far more than accidental. The self-contradictory poses, the centrism, the productive anomalies, the past made new, the traditional made odd, the search for center from which to launch eccentric experiment, the epic-making canons, all suggest that the model for these originals is the Promethean Titan. The model would not please any one of them unless it included another contradictory disguise of the working stiff, not always getting it right but getting it written/made/composed. As with the Whitman and Holmes (or Irving) images, all three would be loath to give up completely either Titan or working stiff in order to adopt fully the other. The art is Promethean. It is also very human, wants to appear to be workaday and very American. Faulkner, Ford, and Ives found identities for American music/film/fiction as distinct as Emerson's clarion call had envisioned, but ones Emerson never knew to hope for because their work also found a new identity for *American* art. All found structures, modes, and forms in the tradition and endowed them with rhythmic and dissonant infarction from their heads or from their genius or from that instrument constructed by each in his own eccentric, center-seeking, pushy, genial, human-loving way. Or by their attempts at community or their appeals to genre.

It seems their experiment is now over. That is another affinity. There have been plenty of imitators of Ford and Faulkner but few successful followers in these experiments. Ives is a special case: what was felt to be his inaccessibility made imitation difficult. Over and done with and we shall not see their like again. Their modes are now, perhaps, even unpopular. Feeling should be, I suppose, kept out of criticism. But one measure of these geniuses, in a complex way the result of all I have tried to adduce here, is that they and their music, film, and fiction care about people. Ford cares more about people than you or I do. So does Faulkner. And so, in that distant and diffident way, does Ives. We must want to try to understand an art which cares so deeply and so originally and is made into so immediate a device for caring. And if we shall not see their like again, how much more critical that understanding of them and what they did becomes.

THREE

COMMUNITY

I have suggested some affinities of Faulkner, Ford, and Ives: a social affinity; that each is a regionalist; and that each seems to have thrived in a common ambivalence of role and image; each is preoccupied by the past; each creates a large body of work; each is a regionalist working in overtly American material; each has a canon which demands to be seen as a whole and bears a structure that could not be the product of accidental accumulation; and each depends on a convention-dominated, conservative-seeming sort of innovation. Here I want to suggest these artists' variations upon a common subject matter.

Faulkner, Ford, and Ives base their work in some form or other of community: for Faulkner it is constant background and, I think, central theme; for Ford it is causal and rhythmic matrix: it determines what happens and how that moves, whether lynching or dance. For Ives social encounter and the massing of people is the root of his music's force and frequently the key to its sometimes puzzling aim. But I mean to discuss community as something more than theme. I had a roommate once who said that Graham Greene's *The Power and the Glory* didn't show him much because, after all, what did it tell him about Mexico? I argued then that I didn't much care what it told me about Mexico as long as it behaved like a novel. Unless the work is doing something besides telling us about Mexico it's not very responsive to critical reading, and even if its telling us about Mexico has some further point, I am still likely to become restive or nod off if it takes too long to get around to it. Community, though, is different from this and more than theme. For these three artists community is central to the formal, structural, temporal, narrative, and spatial relationships I believe fundamental to the understanding of the films of Ford, fiction of Faulkner, music of Ives, and offers as well an acute insight into some issues of canon, convention, and innovation.

Community is such a square subject for innovators. And

again, so American. One has only to cite the Sunday Morning Sequence of Ford's *My Darling Clementine*[1] and imagine for it an audience of three—Faulkner, Ives, and Ford himself—to demonstrate how community transcends theme and to recognize the common ground community calls up for all of them. Of that sequence Ives would like the way the sound comes to us before we know what it is telling us—the hymn we hear as the couple walks down the porch, the church as we imagine it before we see it, and the church's frame as finally shown in the anti-perspectival placement its American flags make of that odd angle at the end of the street; the shift between prayer and foot-stomping fiddle-player; the repetition of Wyatt's slow approach to the church as his brothers make their rather quicker approach to the dance in their buckboard. Faulkner would like the people, trivial and important, and the way they move toward the church; he would like the concentric movement. In *The Hamlet*'s spotted-horses sale he has made a gathering similarly dependent upon shifting rhythms, moods, movements, approaches, participants—a grand dance of this kind but beyond this as another of John Ford's masterful dances— the best and most complete of his several non-commissioned officers' balls (in *Fort Apache*)—is beyond this. And Faulkner would like (and has in his own work matched) the fully functioning world all this implies just beyond the edge of what we see, just out of sight.

The audience of three, Faulkner, Ford, and Ives, would nod assent to what they watched on the screen: Faulkner for the import and force and movement of the sequence; Ives for its sound and space and distances; Ford reflectively and reflexively approving his own work and the way this short passage functions as centerpiece and as commentary on the whole that contains it, at once its balancing point and the validation of the whole of *My Darling Clementine*, establishing so neatly and in such brief compass that this Western means more than it says. Among other things, it means, quite simply, that here is this civilized midst in the vast surround of that favorite of

Ford's many open spaces, Monument Valley. Faulkner might well be impatient with the rest of the movie, Ives might despair simply at being made to sit down in front of a screen (we don't know enough about Ives and the movies), but all three would know their commonplace of association here at this balancing point.

When I refer to Faulkner's feelings about community are not what we might expect, or even what we have assumed. They are as unconventional as his feelings, structures, and shapes for family. Absent mother, invisible father, dominant sister, and feminized son may characterize many of Faulkner's families, but all this doesn't correspond very closely either to the ideal American family of our pious hopes or even to the doomed prototype put forth by a lot of Faulkner criticism. What we expect is not what we get.

When I refer to Faulkner's "idea of" community I must address two issues: his ideal—what he tells us community ought to be at its best—and his depiction of Yoknapatawpha's communities. But Faulkner's depiction of community doesn't come out very conventional either; certainly it doesn't set up an ideal Southern community (either of the New South or the Old). This doesn't mean he didn't think an ideal was possible, one in which the community's people care about and support others according to agreed-upon standards. Faulkner may well have hoped for that and some of his characters may seem to aspire to that. But I suspect rather that our model for an ideal of community is askew, so that the instruments we use to measure the principles of Faulkner's communities may be askew as well. The new realities of international interdependence have shifted my understanding of community and I now read Faulkner with more energy than I could bring to the task when I was in the latter stages of writing the book called *Faulkner's Narrative*. Some of that now seems rushed and I'd like to amend it; but I'll stand by this much on the subject of Faulkner and community.

Of Faulkner's most constant themes—inheritance, possession, guilt—the strongest perhaps are those of isolation and community. The two run throughout the canon, frequently opposed to each other, as I have indicated in the several discussions of *us* and *them*. The completion of this pattern by the later work might best be exemplified by contrasting some characters: say, Emily Grierson and V. K. Ratliff. . . . If Caddy is set beside Emily and Lucius Priest beside V. K., perhaps the point is clearer. The contrast defines opposite poles, the isolated individual and the representative of community, the laconic and the chatty, the doomed woman and the child. . . . Concern for *them* reaches an apex in *Light in August*. . . . The lonely ones tend to be aberrations: they demonstrate by how they differ from us what we share in common with them. The community-figures are norms: in their resemblance to us they demonstrate our desire to depart from their norms. As I have suggested, the isolated ones are not good Tellers. In their mouths first-person narrative is distorted . . . or fragmentary and poetic. . . . The community figures are natural Tellers; telling is a part of the norm they represent, telling about the isolated ones is self-protective for them, as well as a part of their identity, their currency, and frequently their power. Our adoption of the norm they establish . . . is the aim of their telling, and it follows that this . . . norm . . . constitutes a threat to our individuality. What we hold in common with them of group ideal, misconception, myth—or more important, what they *cause us* to hold in common with them—constitutes a failure of our individual uniqueness.[2]

Playing off *us* against *them* is still for me at the heart of Faulkner: and how well the *us* or the *them* can know or tell what is at issue in any particular confrontation is frequently a fit measure of his or their power: How much less does Joe Christmas know of what he's up against as compared to what the Reverend Hightower knows in *Light in August*? What are the effects on Darl of isolation compared to the effects on Dewey Dell in *As I Lay Dying*? The questions are not just who wins and who loses but who will sink forever and who will return to tell the tale.

The most pessimistic of the communities depicted are those

in *Sanctuary* and *Light in August*. I have to make some careful allusions as reminders of these books' virulence. In *Sanctuary* the group examining Tommy's body:

Yet on Monday they were back again, most of them, in clumps about the courthouse and the square, and trading a little in the stores since they were here, in their khaki and overalls and collarless shirts. All day long a knot of them stood about the door to the undertaker's parlor, and boys and youths with and without schoolbooks leaned with flattened noses against the glass, and the bolder ones and the younger men of the town entered in twos and threes to look at the man called Tommy. He lay on a wooden table, barefoot, in overalls, the sun-bleached curls on the back of his head matted with dried blood and singed with powder, while the coroner sat over him, trying to ascertain his last name. But none knew it, not even those who had known him for fifteen years about the countryside, nor the merchants who on infrequent Saturdays had seen him in town, barefoot, hatless, with his rapt, empty gaze and his cheek bulged innocently by a peppermint jawbreaker. For all general knowledge, he had none.[3]

In the same novel, the crowd gathers around the explosion of the flaming victim in the lynching.[4] Both are crowds as unknowing and uncaring as the musing marble of the dead tranquil queens in the Luxembourg Gardens of that novel's unforgettable end:

In the pavilion a band in the horizon blue of the army played Massenet and Scriabine, and Berlioz like a thick coating of tortured Tschaikovsky on a slice of stale bread, while the twilight dissolved in wet gleams from the branches, onto the pavilion and the sombre toadstools of umbrellas. Rich and resonant the brasses crashed and died in the thick green twilight, rolling over them in rich sad waves. Temple yawned behind her hand, then she took out a compact and opened it upon a face in miniature sullen and discontented and sad. . . . She closed her compact and from beneath her smart new hat she seemed to follow with her eyes the waves of music, to dissolve into the dying brasses, across the pool and the opposite semicircle of trees where at sombre intervals the dead tranquil queens in

stained marble mused, and on into the sky lying prone and vanquished in the embrace of the season of rain and death.[5]

In *Light in August* the terms indicting collective humanity become more specific. Here there is an individual villain in
Percy Grimm, the militaristic vigilante, but he is used chiefly
to examine the community collaboration which makes a Percy
Grimm possible. He may well be Faulkner's prophecy of the
SS, but at the same time he is all too American. He has come
too late for the Great War, and must languish as an officer
without an army until his colder ardor shames the town into
begging him to take command of it. But Grimm without this
supportive mob would be nothing. Faulkner further anatomizes septic community in what he sees of the crowd assembled at the burning Burden house: "the sheriff . . . the casual Yankees and the poor whites and even the Southerners
who had lived for a while in the north . . . the hatless men,
who had deserted counters and desks, . . . some of them with
pistols already in their pockets began to canvass about for
someone to crucify."[6]

The community's unity—even its entity—is provided only
by the fire. The emblem of the town's minimal entity and its
collective concern is the snappy fire engine, representing the
societal protection town government will offer even the most
rudimentary communities: shiny and bright, evidently not too
useful. Faulkner anatomizes further: for us to say that this community comes into being only through violence—that these
individuals become an entity only when brought out of their
privatistic lives by the fire—is simplistic. He reminds us that
all these people are idealists; they need to believe, to have
something to believe in. They don't just want somebody to
punish, they want somebody to crucify.

Because the other made nice believing. Better than the shelves and
the counters filled with longfamiliar objects bought, not because the
owner desired them or admired them, or could take any pleasure in
the owning of them, but in order to cajole or trick other men into

buying them at a profit; and who must now and then contemplate both the objects which had not yet sold and the men who could buy them but had not yet done so, with anger and maybe outrage and maybe despair too.[7]

As if that were not enough, this passage goes on to discuss lawyers and doctors and women. As individuals the citizens practice their specialties, each his own, storekeeping or farming or lawyering or doctoring, but each hates the practice in its own terms. All long for a release like this present one of the fire, the momentary unity, the brief distraction and illusion of oneness. They will foster new beliefs, even invent new things to believe in if that is what it takes to be able to continue this substitute for their dull, decaying, and frustrated individual lives. If group action is a product of individuals, Faulkner suggests, it is not just of blind or merely reacting individuals: it is the believing and the dedicated—and most especially the idealistic—individuals we have to look out for. This is a septic community by virtue of the purity of its ideals and the intensity of its individuals' beliefs.

The other side of the coin—the benign community—is depicted in Faulkner in several kinds. The simplest perhaps is the befogged collective first-person narrator of "A Rose for Emily." The narrator contrasts itself—the dominant *we*—to "some of the women," "some of the others," and is not satisfied until at the end of the story it breaks down the door and sees for itself what its (or rather, *our*) benign attention and hereditary care have made of Emily Grierson. The narrative presence skips from subgroup to subgroup within this community like Eliza on the ice floes, pitting this belief against that, making a whole community out of momentary and fragmentary supposes. A stronger good is found in the Trilogy. There is a similar *us*-group, the largely uninformed but generally concerned group on the gallery of *The Hamlet*, sitting there, taking it all in, making it all fit until the Platonic Guardians of the sequel *The Town* come along and make a profession out of watching members of the Snopes family, seeing what each of them is up to, and then the Guardians make of "bush-shaking" detection a kind of defense against the interlopers, the Snopeses.

Community as depicted is a poor guide to the ideal. Of course it was never put there to be an ideal. Community in "Emily" is in that story as a necessary narrative function: the first-person plural of the *we* in this story is essential to the shock with which we find that strand of iron-gray hair at the end of the story and all that attends it. The community accomplishes the isolation of Emily which brings on her awful love and also completes our complicity in this and in the breaking-down of her bedroom door. The mob in *Light in August* is in that novel as enforcement for the (essentially thematic) tracing there of evil's origins; the mob in *Sanctuary* is a function of the indifference of both nature and society to human injustice. The closest to an ideal community depicted in Faulkner is the community set forth in several different ways in the Trilogy. That of *The Hamlet* represents a rather placid plenitude, the rhythm of a give-and-take, live-and-let-live interaction seen, for instance, in the sale of the spotted horses, a depiction of community which becomes almost like one of the group movements in John Ford's films, a grand dance of the living.

Save for the clerk in the background, they were the only two standing, and now, in juxtaposition, you could see the resemblance between them—a resemblance intangible, indefinite, not in figure, speech, dress, intelligence; certainly not in morals. Yet it was there, but with this bridgeless difference, this hallmark of his fate upon him: he would become an old man; Ratliff, too: but an old man who at about sixty-five would be caught and married by a creature not yet seventeen probably, who would for the rest of his life continue to take revenge upon him for her whole sex; Ratliff, never. The boy was moving without haste up the road. His hand rose again from his pocket to his mouth.[8]

The community in *The Town* is a combine of collective concern and self-satisfied justification of the forms-that-be set against would-be interlopers, the profiteering Snopeses.

But he saw it now. Not to destroy the bank itself, wreck it, bring it down about De Spain's ears like Samson's temple, but simply to move it still intact out from under De Spain. Because the bank stood for money. A bank was money, and as Ratliff said, he would never injure money, cause to totter for even one second the parity and immunity of money; he had too much veneration for it. He would simply move the bank and the money it represented and stood for, out from under De Spain, intact and uninjured and not even knowing it had been moved, into a new physical niche in the hegemony and economy of the town, leaving De Spain high and dry with nothing remaining save the mortgage on his house which (according to Ratliff) he had given old Will Varner for the money with which to restore what Byron Snopes had stolen.[9]

Finally, though, begins the decay of such collective certainties and the moral and narrative surenesses of these noble guardians as their function as narrators starts running up against their freedom as protagonists: the puppets become mixed up by tugging their own strings. The narrative in *The Mansion* sometimes depicts an advanced state of this narrator/participant confusion as to role. In this passage Linda is talking, and Gavin does the thinking.

"We were here. Used it. I mean, for the earth to have come all this long way from the beginning of the earth, and the sun to have come all this long way from the beginning of time, for this one day and minute and second out of all the days and minutes and seconds, and nobody to use it, no two people who are finally together at last after all the difficulties and waiting, and now they are together at last and are desperate because of all the long waiting, they are even running along the beach toward where the place is, not far now, where they will finally be alone together at last and nobody in the world to know or care or interfere so that it's like the world itself wasn't except you so now the world that wasn't even invented yet can begin."

And I thinking *Maybe it's the fidelity and the enduring which must be so at least once in your lifetime, no matter who suffers. That you have heard of love and loss and grief and fidelity and enduring and you have seen love and loss and grief but not all five of them since the fidelity and enduring I am speaking of were inextricable: one*—this, even while she was saying, "I don't mean just—" and stopped herself before I could have raised the hand to clap on to her lips—if I had been going to.[10]

Somehow now both Mink and Flem seem all too human (to say nothing of Gavin seeming all too fallible) for our earlier impressions to hold.

Perhaps we are all so certain of Faulkner's authorial distance from all this that it would never occur to us to identify any of these depicted communities as his *ideal* of community. But I think it has occurred to most of us to tag the weakest of the lot—the increasingly defensive ideal of community responsibility espoused by Chick, V. K., and Gavin in *The Town* and *The Mansion*—as Faulkner's own. I think this is in error and that this benignant ideal is perhaps, of any of the communities, the least what it appears to be. It poses as community conscience, it postures about as consensus struggling toward what is right, communal responsibility crying to be born. It is nothing of the kind.

I argued in *Faulkner's Narrative* that Faulkner's ideal of community *is* this orderly Apollonian rule of Right Thing, Right Measure, Our Kind of Behavior, which the Guardians of Jefferson set up in *The Town*.[11] They (that is, the Snopeses, that dream version of *them*) are coming, but *we* in our own quiet way will be able to resist by dint of being prepared, like a group of well-schooled Faulkner boy scouts. Not only do I no longer think this is Faulkner's ideal, I'm not even sure it's community. I think when Gavin stands on the hillside in *The Mansion* and looks down on His Town in the manner of Thornton Wilder's Stage Manager, he is not representing Faulkner's ideal of community; when the outsiders (such as Moseley and MacGowan) watch the progress of the Bundrens, they are not Faulkner's ideal of community; the gallery group in *The Ham-*

let may exemplify a part of that ideal but by no means embody it. And certainly the Unholy Alliance of Gavin, V. K., and Chick do not. Community is not vigilantes: it is an ideal. But when we state ideal I think our tendency is to turn moral and—worse—proscriptive and punitive. We long as surely to be winners in *The Town* and *The Mansion* as we do to be door-breakers in "A Rose for Emily." And with some of the same convicting results.

A Chinese student from the Peoples' Republic said he did not understand how Americans learned that they must toler-ate the religion of other Americans; or, if they had learned this, how the Americans could then be brought to do it. The question parallels, I think, Faulkner's understanding of an ideal of community. Why should we expect that all the mem-bers of a community even know it exists, much less acknowl-edge it by intent or action? The law applies to all but when we say "the law"—as abstracted from its particulars—we Ameri-cans can mean the sheriff with the badge, not the mass of farmers, ranchers, Indians, schoolmarms, whores, and care-free lads and lasses to whom the law is *the* law. Just so with community. Individuals take actions for it that it cannot take itself—they take them on behalf of the whole, but there is no reason to think the whole even knows what is being done in its behalf, much less accedes to it or collaborates with them in taking the actions.

Whenever someone proclaims Community Belief or Com-munity Standards or even Communal Interest, count your sil-ver: it's time to look out; the proclaiming folks are probably up to no good. It's not hard to identify the true community that lies behind some individual actions in the Trilogy: V. K. nails up the clapboard on the stable in *The Hamlet* to cut short the raree-show enterprise of those who would have profited from and those who would have watched the feeble-minded Ike Snopes and his beloved cow. Eula gets a tombstone bought by the Guardians. The collaborative CIA formed by V. K., Gavin, and Chick is not true community, nor is any of that strawberry-ice-cream business between Gavin and Linda (Eula Varner's daughter). But it's just possible that for reasons both of charity and commonweal the shipping of the Snopes Indian children back west *is* community. In other words, community is what we all know to be the common good but what so few of us have the will, the freedom, or the genius to act correctly for—in its spirit, by its command, in its behalf. Elitist standards and individual needs tend to get in our way. To say nothing of the rule of mobs, the power of storm-trooper leadership, ennui, neglect, and, as Boswell says, the "forgetfulness of things years after their happening, and such dreary truths."[12] Faulkner in the Trilogy at first reminds us that the gathering of individuals without higher guide or with the *wrong* higher guide is a social evil; but then that the attempt to band together to halt the activities of the interlopers can become an equal wrong: it is ultimately isolative both of *us* and of *them*. Both sides of the coin as tossed fail of the high ideal and the hard rule of community: individuals willing and acting in the stead of a whole which cannot itself take actions.

It is just possible that the fading light of community as depicted in *The Mansion* was for Faulkner the fading light of common day. I don't mean *The Mansion* is his *Tempest* or that Faulkner considered how his light had failed, but rather that *The Mansion* stood to the canon as the story "Go Down, Moses" stands to the novel of that name: this last novel of the Trilogy is coda, casting the fortune of a gloomy future. The Supreme Court got itself into a bind using concepts of "community" in its obscenity rulings because it may well be that, as with oaths and sacred affirmations, too few people any longer believed in them for them to be able to bear up under the pressure of a legal test. Community is like "tradition" in Canon Law, subject to the contemporary interpretation of the authority's belief that it (tradition) exists and in its belief in itself (authority). The problem is one of both intensity and spread. Do we think we are, as a whole nation, still a community? Is there anything in our towns or cities or villages or blocks—or

even, God wot, in our universities—we can still call community? Where did we lose it and when? *The Mansion* may well,
at least for Faulkner's canon, toll its passing knell.

If one were to have to choose but one word to characterize
the subject of Ford's total canon, community would be a more
appropriate word than any other I can think of: certainly more
so than hero or people or family or cavalry or even service,
duty, or honor; and more appropriate, too, than any adjective—more than American or Western or dynamic or placid
or concerned or loving or caring. One-word characterization
would be, as my examples suggest, silly: simple and brutal injustice and insufficiency. But the important thing is, community is less insufficient than other words.

To know what Ford thought community was is of course far
more difficult than just to assert that he made it central. It is
even difficult to be sure *how* he understood it. I think he
knows community (and makes us know it) in terms of movement and containment, the same terms in which his movies
always ultimately resolve our attitudes, allegiances, and conclusions. Such movements are never simple, but involve light
and dark, shadow and substance, force and passivity, confluence and dispersion, rhythm and chance. Approaches and
departures are as important (as demonstrated by the Sunday
Morning Sequence and all of the dances) as the celebration or
recognition or realization of the community itself. So what
Ford thought community was might well be approached first in
a thematic and then in an exemplary examination: the thematic an attempt to test representative movies as they present
issues of community; the exemplary by examining those most
formal of all the many formal occasions in Ford's work: the
dances, balls, hoedowns, and social sashays that thread all the
way through his movies.

The most interesting communities in Ford's work fall between *Stagecoach* (1939) and *Seven Women* (1966), films which

themselves might be thought of as a great parenthesis to the main range of development of the canon as a whole as well as to the comings-together and flyings-apart which seem to make Ford's communities in general.[13] *Stagecoach* presents I suppose Ford's most imitated and most representative community, a happenstance assemblage of types thrown together in a desert *Pequod*, moving across a highly charged and (finally) almost totally abstracted landscape toward the dubious Promised Land of Lordsburg. As this community makes its progress it not only gathers its constituent members but settles some values, and the stops along the way give this abstraction, this floating community, social dimensions. The progress ends in Lordsburg with the dissipation of the stagecoach community in the subjection of its standards to the community standards of the town, arrest, gunfight, perhaps death.

Seven Women is (in contrast to this) a classic closed enclave with its conventional and habitual assumptions.[14] Everybody in the place could use some sleep and a little fresh air: they've been knocking up against each other for too long. Fresh elements are then introduced to this closed world and have to be integrated and perhaps absorbed if either enclave or individuals are to survive. The exposition of all this is less carefully "motivated" in conventional dramaturgical terms than in *Stagecoach* (surprisingly so, since *Stagecoach* is such an abstract film) and the working-out of how to resolve old with new is in its development less conclusive, more authoritarian, and far more problematic than in the earlier picture. But *Seven Women* is, as clearly as *Stagecoach* is, resolved in movement, light and shadow, gathering and dispersion. No longer is the context Monument Valley, no longer is the characteristic movement the grand circular meanderings of horses and stagecoach mounting in a spiral for a climactic rush to Lordsburg, but people inside a missionary compound, locked at their dinner table and in their bedrooms and offices, their movement reduced to caged pacings. Indoors pressure concentrates these smaller movements by sealing them off from relief from the outside world. The outdoors only exists in *Seven Women* by virtue of sound-stage tricks.[15] Yet the interior pressure continually implies and alludes to an outside world exploding with menace and revolution. The pressure outside comes inside as the bandit horde takes over the compound and the mix of old inside and new inside produces powerful and ever-more-claustrophobic social abstractions. The person-to-person contracts, exchanges, bargains, and face-offs are more mature and more sophisticated than any of the relationships in *Stagecoach* in their accomplished sense of the complexity, compromise, and cost of human encounter and sacrifice. So a rather unprepared-for action takes place in a distanced social situation, and as might be expected in such a mix the result is a certain enigma. In all this turning and shifting and recasting, it is very hard to catch up and Ford I think doesn't want us to. *Stagecoach* too has its abstractions—of movement, rhythm, and especially the shadows of the way-station interiors and of the carefully framed and edited interior spaces of the stagecoach. But there when our head spins with violent reduction and abstraction we can rest on the bosom of sure and reassuring melodrama. The gun to the head of the pregnant woman is one of the most powerful and disturbing single shots and one of the most remarkable *coups* I know in film, but the most innocent moviegoer could hardly fail to interpret what he sees pretty well. It is sure melodrama.

Menace and risk are so much more abstracted in *Seven Women* than in *Stagecoach* that it is hard for us to participate in them. Individuals are more nearly souls laid bare, but the reasons for this baring as well what might be the further issue of such revelation lack the clear (by comparison, melodramatic) motivation and cause and effect of *Stagecoach*. So we may make the error of giving up on the missionary compound as too distant or simply baffling. There's another trouble with this community: the communal action here (like some similar actions in Faulkner) is taken by a single individual: Doctor D. R. Cartwright (Anne Bancroft) alone. The others understand, or fail to understand, or reject her astonishing vicarious atonement, but they don't *do* it or even collaborate in it. In other words, we see here at its purest an individual who sees the community ideal (alone) and takes her action on the community's behalf (alone). Our understanding of this action—which might itself otherwise be impossibly distanced—is enabled by a generic inheritance from other movies. Doctor Cartwright's arrival at the compound in her riding habit with her professional ways not only sets up an impending conflict with the head missionary—we have seen this before and we will again—but the riding trousers, the stance, and the manner also make us know we are already familiar with her personal history of settlements and resolutions, raising the ante on what the Doctor's sacrifice must be when the time comes. We know by watching her at work that she has been able to commit herself to this work only by ignoring and riding roughshod over the fools she finds around her; that her commitment is not to the people she serves and heals, but is rather commitment to commitment: riding roughshod has become an integral part of the spiritual income—the little self-indulgence she counts on as part of her payment for doing what she does well. But when the time comes for her sacrifice—that astonishingly uncharacteristic sacrifice—how right that it is offered for people she cannot stand to be with, how complete that it must be undertaken in the silken disguise of a courtesan, she who will not use her woman's front name, how absolute that the sacrifice must be completely irrelevant to all that is inherent in her chosen work save only the selflessness.

How do we know all this? Partly by the concentration and focus of just those restricted and severe interior spaces Ford has made of the courtyard, the offices, the consultation room, and the dinner table. By the way this concentration forces us to stare at faces. By the way Ford has established new and separated spaces to enclose the other women. By the Doctor's formal garbing of herself in the outlandish courtesan garb and by the way we watch her doing so as Ford has devised for us to watch it. If it is difficult to rationalize in language the visual art by which Ford gives us Monument Valley, how much more difficult to articulate the personal readings and experiencings he has devised to force us into these interior landscapes.

Between these two very different abstracted worlds and their very different communities—a parenthesis of extremes— is a world of Ford communities—good, bad, neutral—but none that goes farther than *Stagecoach* in the complexity of abstracted motion, none that goes beyond *Seven Women* in the involution and complexity of the interaction between depicted personal exchange and the personal cinema John Ford has devised to enable it.

Community in Faulkner is complicated because family and jailhouse and barbershop take on an entity and essence independent of community, each in its dynamics differing from his perhaps more proscribed and delimited essence of community. But in Ford, family, service unit, and enclave are all communal. The essence of all is people together. In Faulkner the essence of a family relationship—sexual union, parent, child— in part defines itself by being played off against the essence of the social relationship of the community. That of a fighting unit in Faulkner is significant only in the World War I stories, but that of a sealed-off enclave sometimes becomes distinctive from all others as the operative shape that social relationship and association take to find their function ("Dry September," "Lo!," Quentin and Shreve's Harvard in *Absalom, Absalom!*). In Ford, in that all this can be reduced to movement, gesture, confluence, and dispersion, the military unit (as in *The Horse Soldiers*) is a type of community and something of a family; the family in *The Grapes of Wrath* and *Fort Apache*, but not, I think, in *How Green Was My Valley* becomes a segment of community—more significant as community than as family insofar as it works to unite individual motions and to express common standards.

To measure the distance between *Stagecoach* and *Seven Women*, though, we need more than a formal argument, because between them has fallen World War II. The two great film artists of community are Ford and Frank Capra. World War II represents for either a fork in the road and for Capra the decision is never really made, the road not taken. *It's a Wonderful Life, State of the Union, A Hole in the Head,* and *Pocketful of Miracles* adhere to the belief and principles which enabled his masterpieces of the Thirties and Forties but by this time the underpinnings of these principles as well as any connection they may have had to our world are gone. The fit analogy is perhaps that of fantasy, the believable impossible. The community of *It's a Wonderful Life* may survive unchanged from *Mr. Deeds Goes to Town,* but what has departed is *our* automatic belief in that community and the bridge between these films and the world we inhabit, which this belief, before the war at least, made possible. The gloom, pessimism, and fantastic abstract filmic power of Capra's films has always been underestimated. But most critics have at the same time overestimated the connections between his worlds and the world of our lives. By the time of *It's a Wonderful Life,* divorce between the two is complete.

Ford shifts gears in the films made in the late Forties and seems by the time of these pictures to have known that what has been will be no more. He manages to include the postwar failure of community and our belief in that failure (rather than our belief in the community). His films seem to take this as a given, to treat the decay of our belief in the common set of ideals that community embodied as if it were no more out of the way than another horse or cactus. He makes the transition to an unbelieving communal world, a new world of interdependency. And to what we are as we return from World War II. In what I have to say of community that follows, I am attempting to be true to this broader sense of community as Ford evolved it, that new, far more complicated sense of people together—post-community America—which makes possible the moral structure of his films after the war.

The Horse Soldiers is a movie of pivotal definitive moments, moments of essence, and in some of these the nature of the cavalry unit comes to the fore.[16] The most significant comes as the troop marches out of camp near the beginning of the movie; another comes just before this, as they are gathered in the camp; later as the unit turns into the swamp; as it waits in silence for the Confederate troops to pass by on the other side of the river; as it awaits the onslaught (and finally retreats in the face) of the boys of the military school; as it gathers at the amputation, or to present Hannah Hunter with the looking glass. All these are communal. But as the cavalry unit at the rail junction awaits the more threatening, half-crazed charge of the Confederate troops, banners flying, and again (near the movie's end) as it charges the cannon emplacement across the bridge, the group becomes a fighting unit, a piece of army. The question remains whether these two—community and fighting unit—differ from each other. But even in these passages we continue to recognize the men we know and our point of view is so thoroughly within their force that we never have the distance from them to think of them as a run-of-the-mill army (except perhaps as they wreck the railroad and destroy the rails), but they are not in these passages clearly communal. In the communal association dependency, hierarchy, rivalries and spats and loyalties, the functions and dynamic balances, speak of community. The measure of the film's power is its ability to convince us of the audience—even though we may never have been of an army or a part of a fighting unit, or combatant at all—that its issues of war and peace are ours. So in a sense both communal and noncommunal passages operate on the audience in a communal engagement. We in the audience are of the community the movie forms even when it doesn't extend to many of the folks on the screen. Military unit as community is one of Ford's most fundamental structures: that mutual dependence is so essential for survival strips all other concerns to their essentials.

The Wings of Eagles widens this shape to depict the military as a worldwide community by showing us a small segment and multiplying this by means of newsreel and headline and dialogue to suggest a small-town shape spread thin over the whole world: everybody knows everybody else through thick and thin, various transfers back and forth, good duty and bad, ashore and at sea. The navy and everybody in it manage to keep track of their own.[17] In short, the peacetime navy. The worldwide community has always been a fiction, but in the peacetime navy between the wars it was probably less fictional than we might think. What the movie strives for in this small-town format has a basis in fact, for at this time nobody in the army or navy was paid when or what he was supposed to be paid, everybody had heard of everybody else because the bulk of the officers were from the academies. Possible duty stations were few, and the world—this world at least—was small. All this *bonhomme* community is set against the rather less balanced and certainly less harmonious domestic grouping made up of diminishing returns: loss of child, failure of marital exchange, and decay and escape in drink. *Rio Grande*[18] assumes something like this kind of world as a given and sets against it (not so much to be a piece of it as to be a departure from its rules) the stormy marriage of its two principals (John Wayne and Maureen O'Hara), a couple all in the service have heard of, who bring with them an almost legendary memory (as seen in O'Hara's grudge against Victor McLaglen). Some of this context of worldwide neighborhood Ford must have borrowed from a common empathy device of films of the late Thirties and Forties. In *White Heat*[19] another master of the enclave, Raoul Walsh, has a world in which not only have all the crooks heard of all the other crooks, but they know the cops and the screws and the wardens as well, nationwide. Talk about your organized crime: crime in that movie is organized like the U.S. Senate. So with the officers'-club navy of *The Wings of Eagles*. Community here seems to be described as something not much different from a state of mind or a world view.

Of all Ford's military communities, the one in *They Were Expendable* is the most carefully articulated and fully structured.[20] Community is the form, the essence, narrative, and substance of this movie. And every bit of it is visualized. What we see at the end of the movie states formally an almost familial outfit, still military in its rules (John Wayne cannot disobey orders and hunt for Donna Reed; Ward Bond, the superior petty officer remaining behind in the Islands, receives Montgomery's binoculars from him), but communal in virtually every other regard. Wayne and Montgomery are returning to the States in the last plane, leaving behind officers from other units whose allusions speak again of that *Wings of Eagles* world in which everybody knows everybody else. As this last plane roars away overhead, the remainder of the force, the family, the unit, this part of the damaged community limps away along the beach, having been deprived first of their fighting function, then even of mail duty, then of their boat, then (they are now attached to the army) of their service, then of their officers, and now finally of the direct control of any superior officers. Their orders are to get to the mountains and fight on. The final title card tags all this with MacArthur's "We Shall Return," again acknowledging a larger community beyond our sight, but the dislocation and pain of what we see—because it rests on such a powerful dynamic of developed images—stays with us longer than the ring of that tag line.

The stockade has been extended first to a base, then to the size of an island, then an island group, then an ocean, then a force. But many of the actions persist from the stockade shape; the dance at Corregidor has a front porch like the stockade building in *Fort Apache* and that in *Two Rode Together*; the old boatyard owner has a jug and a shotgun; the candlelight dinner has a surrogate Sons of the Pioneers (like *Rio Grande* or *Wagon Master*) and the touch of home where men are formal, and women are pretty and feminine and wear pearls. All this is more than togetherness of association or huddling together for warmth: its articulate exchange and the reciprocated force of the feelings apparent in this world make possible the full function of the life of a community. *Expendable* is perhaps the best of Ford's military communities for another reason, too: it takes a unit which hasn't yet invented its use or proved its worth ("those little boats") and develops its primary function, proves this function in battle even as we are being introduced to the men of the unit as, in another movie, we might be introduced to the members of a family. It is an almost perfectly coordinated coming together as participants become known and come together one by one, even as the community begins to find its function and its organic unity, and then an almost complete falling apart as the individuals die and boats sink or fall away or are carried off through the jungle by the army, and the community disperses and decays. What is implied by what we see (not necessarily, as I have said, by "We Shall Return"), what we know of World War II, or what the movie's words tell us is that the larger community (the navy, the country) is falling apart a little faster than the PT unit in which Ford makes us take so great an interest. As our group finds its use and hits its stride, it already knows that the old *Arizona* will never again for them come steaming up that now so empty channel, and the dissipation of our unit is still to come. The poignancy of the exemplary decay revealed throughout this losing battle of a movie is all the more strong in that we know where we are in this war: this story comes at a time in the war which will doom the unit. Only the larger communal memory residual in the survivors of the smaller community will give it any survival at all.[21]

Stockade is, I suppose, the paradigm community of Ford's films, and the paradigm instance of stockade is *Drums Along the Mohawk*.[22] I bring it so late to this discussion deliberately because I think the movie—like *Stagecoach*—is too frequently dismissed as simplistic, so that showing a need in the argument for a stockade shape before introducing it seems a good idea. It is more than that and the function of the stockade in the story is an important part of why it is more. The movie is *simple* but in a way which tests all later and more complex versions of its issues and sets the base line for later innovation, development, and variation upon this theme. And the theme frequently, as in *Drums*, seems to depend not just on the community's whole, but on its constituent parts in the smaller communities of family and couple which make it up (*The Wings of Eagles*, *Rio Grande*, *Fort Apache*, *Wagon Master*, *Clementine*, and so on).

Gil and Lana Martin are first shown (in a very nearly wooden job of historic re-creation) at their wedding in Albany, just before setting forth for the wilderness. The woodenness is, I think, as deliberate as the sound-stage treatment of *They Were Expendable*'s last airport—the appropriate treatment for what will become for us the automatic community of Albany, the representative of an unearned civilization, the world later recalled to Lana by her talismans, the china teapot and the peacock feather. The couple comes to its own settlement—cabin, fire, and friendly Indian—and it is difficult to say which of these most terrifies Lana. She responds not just to the shock of the new but to the absence of familiar supports and habitual reciprocation, and the scenes are built so we may feel this with her. Both her shock and what she finds missing, as recounted by the film from her point of view, suggest a risk to the couple's unity.

Their first move toward community, as they sign on as tenants on the Widow McKlennan's farm, is another shock—the burning of their cabin breaks the teapot as surely as it moves them closer to community and the support this new community offers, and this marks the beginning of Lana's independence. First the Widow, then the other good women (not the jealous ones who envy her her nice things) suggest that a unity can be sought by supporting the men. But this has barely been set in motion when the men are taken off to battle. The

Widow McKlennan then observes that the women's unity goes beyond helpmeet subjugation and has more to do perhaps with espousal of abstract female strength, something rather more connected with her distant contemplation of failing males and her love with Barney that used to be as she stares into the fire and mutters, "Barney, Barney." Lana moves across the field following the departing militia column, and this spatial image of the movie's center of unity and the threat departure represents begins to take on societal shape. At their return as Lana calls at intervals in vain along the dragging returning column at night we see the other half of the visual metaphor of marital division and return—lamp in the dark and rain, hope dwindling as the last members of the group straggle by. The battle itself is apparently irrelevant to Ford as an action, but Gil's half-telling of it to his wife is vital as she, more concerned by his wounds, only half-listens; it speaks of another terror and threat which lie just beyond the edge of community, just out of sight.

Community provides little for the birth of the Martins' first child but a chorus of comic support, a kind of comic obbligato of company, community background and support for what has to be done and suffered alone, but which has been suffered before and will be again.

Then the stockade, the siege; Gil leaves again, this time in an attempt to save the whole, in that most incredibly empathetic of all Ford's chases. Gil runs for help pursued by three leaping Mohawks, and Lana adopts the man's role, his blouse, and his musket to defend the stockade as a close-quarters combatant. Finally the comic community (that which is amused at the lying-in, which loves company for an audience, which jokes and plays and makes no demands—Jessie Ralph and Eddie Collins and some others) returns to the fore as Blue Back the Friendly Indian rises in the pulpit of the chapel to show them his trophy of victory over the British, the Englishman's (John Carradine's) eye patch.

The flag-raising at the end extends what we have learned of

community to a national scope, but Gil and Lana simply watch it and then return to those tasks which must give the familial exchange with a community its meaning, the wreaking of sustenance and the making of the life, a smaller earned whole within the now fully earned greater and reunited whole, the shape of community as forged in stockade now enlarged upon the greater counterpart of nation. Albany to this is nothing, because we—and they—never earned Albany. The flag is not what all this has been heading for, but Gil and Lana walking away from it toward their cabin are. No matter what the words have told us, we have been shown and we believe wedding, marriage, family, community, and whole.

All very positive, straightforward, and even nationalistic (although, I would insist again, not jingoistic). Except that this does not account for the fullness of our feelings, our involvement throughout in the people represented by Henry Fonda and Claudette Colbert. And it does not account for the "fishhooks" in this happy blend: the power of Lana's doubts as she shrinks from Blue Back, as she fingers her talismans, as she watches Gil march away, the unsatisfactory (even to herself) stoicism of the Widow McKlennan at the death of General Herkimer; the screams of Joe Boleo (whom we know even less well than the Widow) as he burns on the hay wain. All these represent negative elements of community involvement and are testimony to its great power. It all works instead as does that incredible chase Gil leads the Mohawks across the countryside from dawn to dusk. It is not possible for one white to outrace three Mohawks running at top speed. The tricks of editing, composition, and selective framing used to make this appear plausible are simple and transparent. We know all this and yet we believe. Partly we know we are expected to take a simple explanation, for this movie is making its difficult points so simply. Partly we are seeing it so it must be there. Partly Ford makes it better to believe than not. Forget the exhaustion, the shoes, the log that trips us up, the problems, the thirst: the main line of our hope is to believe in an ideal of the

impossible chance. And this may summarize the distance between military unit and stockade: stockade doesn't achieve its
essence until it is besieged. Then it has resident women (as
most military units do not) and an ultimate test of survival
as siege leads to walled Last Stand awaiting a rescue. And, as
Drums demonstrates, marriage is a stockade.

A critic has said that the moral structure of Hogarth's prints
depends on the hint of an ideal always present, ever so far in
the background. This ideal and idealized world of the happy
stockade is more than a hint, but I would suggest that for
the Ford canon, *Drums Along the Mohawk* provides that constant ideal against which to judge the failures, compromises,
inflexible obsessions, and rigidities of other characters in other
stockades and near-stockades, the other supports that fail, ma-
lign communities and slipped ideals, hints of the serpent in
the garden of married love (*The Wings of Eagles*, *The Man Who
Shot Liberty Valance*, *The Searchers*, *Rio Grande*, *Two Rode Together*, *Seven Women*). This high-water mark is standard, balance, and measuring stick for everything that comes after. In
particular it measures the breaking point following World
War II.

The stockade does not exist except as an idea in *Liberty Valance*, *My Darling Clementine*, or *Wagon Master* (indeed in *My
Darling Clementine* the Clantons seem to be the ones defend-
ing the stockade as they wait at the O.K. Corral). In *Fort
Apache*, *She Wore a Yellow Ribbon*, *Two Rode Together*, and
Seven Women there are literal stockades. These films seem to
form a group because all deal in one way or another with the
role of the individual seen against the common good, the
stockade mentality, the community and how its values are
adopted by an outsider.

My Darling Clementine[23] is, again, a *locus classicus* of the
more direct form of the statement. Wyatt comes to town and
gets good and mad at the drunken Indian and doesn't take the
job, but finds his little brother murdered and does. The tension between peacekeeping law and vengeance law, between

personal vendetta that uses the law as a cover (or, in the case
of the Clantons, personal affront) and the ideal of community
good leading to civilization—a very much abstracted ideal—
is embodied in Wyatt's choice: the physical surroundings of
the movie are its metaphor. The tension Wyatt finds between
individual preference (Doc Holliday is his friend) and legal
obligation (Chihuahua looks as if she knows the killer) sharp-
ens this tension. But in this film the violence of the Clantons
and their barbaric habit of making their own laws as they go
along, the probably corrupt, profit-motivated self-law of the
decaying Holliday, even the comfy assuredness of Wyatt's
gambling, drinking, eating, dancing, law-enforcing, and barbershop habits, together with his savvy, his big gunfighter rep,
and his all-purpose know-how, don't have a chance against
a single overpowering image of the overarching metaphor:
Tombstone on the edge of the abyss, the town lined up geo-
metrically against the massed forms of nature that loom behind it and before it. The place will make the community
come to be and the forces of community are nothing to this.
The show will go on in peace, not just because Doc likes
Shakespeare, but because the community owes the players
some peace and Wyatt will have to fight the rioting townsfolk
if he doesn't deliver the Shakespearean from his captivity in
the saloon. The gunfight at the corral will be pursued not just
for Wyatt's grudge, but because the badge's showdown with
lawlessness is unavoidable. Clementine will stay in town because life goes on and down the street both a church and a
dance are starting. No more than *Drums Along the Mohawk* is
this a community without tears, but it is a center line for the
frontier, as *Drums* is for the stockade, from which the other
communities can diverge, a little less pure than *Drums*, a lot
clearer a world and a social system than those of *Liberty Valance* or *Two Rode Together*, to say nothing of *Seven Women*.

   Wagon Master, like *Stagecoach*, is a floating community—
pacifists (some of them cussing pacifists, the kind of pacifist
group in which it might be predicted that a kid would have a

pistol and slip it to his female kin to hide), to which Ben
Johnson and Harry Carey, Jr. come and cast their lot. The
horse traders' motives and morals are less sure, but less selfish
than Wyatt's.[24] Ben Johnson's horse thieving and his resultant
knowledge of the trails and the way west don't prepare him for
his job and what the wagon train is going to meet as well as
Wyatt's gunfighter rep prepares him for Tombstone and what
threatens it: there's little similar chance for a leisurely shake-
down before the showdown. The wandering band of outlaws
(a very Clanton-like set of Cleggs) here seeks the protection
of the wagon train's community (but for the wrong reason—
protective coloration) as they wait to make their move. A
medicine-show group, impossible cliffs, and shortage of water
add complications. One vision of the film seems to tell us this
is an idyllic outdoors world like Huck Finn's river, but the vi-
gnette which precedes the overture by the Sons of the Pioneers seems to be telling us something quite different. It re-
counts the wounding of Uncle Shiloh and his cold-blooded
murder by shotgun of his assailant. It takes place indoors, our
only venture under a roof in the movie (strangely parallel to
Red River's long venture out of doors and the meeting indoors
finally to set the deal for the cattle.[25] But Ford is never this
simple (or this overtly symbolic). The outdoors is awful, too.
A simple Illyrian reading will not do where the God-fearing
Mormons are thought by the white settlers to have horns and
the Indians regard them as their friends because they don't
cheat as much as other whites. Or where the *vox populi* is an
inarticulate horn, blown alike for "Wagons West" and "Hey
Rube." The community is here a complex ideal of togetherness, oddly mixed in with a need for mutual defense and comparative values (water for shaving and water for drinking;
snake oil for anesthetic and snake oil to drink to survive in the
desert with; dancing for celebration and dancing for mating),
and collective toleration (cussing Elder and Bible-quoting
killer). The stockade moves across the landscape and is, as it
turns out, no defense against the Indians who ask the Mor-

mons to a dance, or against the crooks who simply walk in and take over.

But ironic reflection on elegant complexity is not a proper response to what this movie can show us, and here again we come down to the hard matter of Ford's images, the visual equivalents for the words. This film's words pale when set beside its images. The open spaces of this film are understood by the progress of the wagon train across them: the train defines a rock-lined geometry, its spiraling space ("Didn't we pass that rock a way back?"), and measures its immeasurable distance. We do not know the song of the overture until we move miles away across Monument Valley and look back to hear it come from that distance from the vagrant train. As the space is understood, so are the people known, in familiar Ford shorthand of slightly off-center types: the tart who craves domesticity, but must respond to the horse thief as "that Rube"; the Sister of the Church who casts a lickerish eye. But never so well known as from inside this complex group. We have come to know the train by looking all the way back, from close foreground to deep background (as we do in *The Horse Soldiers* to a different effect). We see not just dialogue scene or anecdotal encounter in the foreground, but the child on the hobbyhorse farther back, causing us to wonder what all must be made to fit into a Conestoga. Then following a dialogue scene comes a similarly deep space in which we think we are seeing no more than Sandy (Harry Carey, Jr.) tipping his hat to the lusty-eyed sister, when his movement across the screen and out of it to the left leaves us without drama to watch and reveals against the camp's dust Sister Ledyard with her horn, Mr. Peachtree (Francis Ford) trying to keep up with his drum, and an unidentified fife player to make up a band of three, piping to no good tune but bravely harmonic, and making a perfect harmony for what we watch. It is one of those lovely discovered orders in Ford's films when there are more layers than we at first thought, like that in which Sergeant Posey (Andy Devine) and Elena (Linda Cristal) stand beside the wagon near the end of *Two Rode Together* and a series of perfect framings falls into place, each achieved in a sequence we marvel at, both as accidental and devised, as one after another person leaves the frame and the frame adjusts to each new grouping and each new remaining space and residual composition. Discovered order is, I think, the essence not only of Ford's individual shots and sequences such as those I have described, but also of the way that Ford's narrative meets and is enforced by his formal structure. Spaces in Ford are understood: the open shapes and scope of Monument Valley and other exteriors, no better than the tight shapings with which Ford forms and by which he re-forms the inside of the coach in *Stagecoach*, the several reinventions of the spaces of the tent interiors in *Two Rode Together*[26] (for Stewart's interviews with the aggrieved family members of the Indian captives) or in *Rio Grande* (for the discussions of the failed father with his son and failed husband with his wife) or the tents in *The Horse Soldiers*, or such formal interiors as the dance space in *Fort Apache* or *Two Rode Together* or as abstracted or apparently non-narrative a space as Hannah Hunter's (Constance Towers's) front room and hall and the exploration Ford makes of it. By the time he finishes with them, we know them in a way far more profound than we do the spaces of our lives, our homes, our work. They have become understood because they have been rationalized and inserted in a time certain, with its own lights and movements and sounds, with that final and definitive experiential power we can only know in Ford. People in Ford are known—and of the several certainties I know, the most certain is that Ford cares more about people than you or I do. Through their walks, their hesitations, we share John Wayne's thoughts or Ward Bond's stares. We know Jane Darwell by what she doesn't say as well as by what she does, by her blowing of the horn (as Sister Ledyard) or her breaking of the eggs for Uncle Shiloh. We don't know these people better than our families, but they are better known by these moments than a member of our family is known by any moment we can isolate in memory: we are more intensely familiar with these because they too have been placed not just in time but in space, certain and fixed forever. Doctor D. R. Cartwright sees herself fully garbed as a courtesan. Lincoln comes to the top of the hill. And Robert Montgomery, in badly cut-off khakis and uniform-issue shoes, stares out a now abandoned channel looking not just for the Old *Arizona* but for the promise. Known people in an understood space. Known and understood in light and movement within a frame.

This may well be the reason Ford returns to some narrative shapes so persistently and it is certainly why he so loves the Western: the shapes—at least for Ford—determine inevitably the spaces. The stagecoach, the PT boat's bridge, the tent, the wagon train, the stockade, Monument Valley, the cavalry line, Hannah Hunter's front room are all understood—and evocative narrative—spaces. The narrative shape or situation demands *and* fits the understood space.

I think that we know endings of John Ford movies—they conclude themselves for us—not when the dramatic conflict is resolved or when the events as plotted draw together to a conclusion, or even, as in a musical composition, when all the material has been rehearsed, developed, and accounted for, but when these known characters have found their proper place in an understood space, or a sequence of such knowns has found repose in a sequence of such physical things understood. Harry Carey, Jr. pursues his lusty come-on out of the frame and we are left with a group which completes those knowns and the spaces understood better than any dramaturgical unit might: three bad musicians making music in the dust. I think this is the reason we are always more tempted to understand Ford and to recount what he has made happen to us in terms of the films' moments, pauses, silences, hesitations, glances, *aperçus*, things we can just barely not describe, rather than in terms of speeches or scenes or exchanges or conflicts or realizations. Wayne on the banks of the *Rio Grande* is not an *anagnorisis* or dramaturgical function of any kind, but it is felt, he is known, and his space has been under-stood. Jane Darwell and her earrings in *The Grapes of Wrath*, Victor Mature with his diploma in *Clementine*, depend on no dramaturgical stuff or placement, any more than does Natalie Wood at the top of the dune in *The Searchers*, John Wayne in the narrow canyon in *Three Godfathers*, or Edna May Oliver before the fire in *Drums Along the Mohawk*. All these are be-yond both realism and dramaturgy. They are film artifice, film visions of the highest order.

Ford's dances complete the pattern of known and under-stood. They are master abstractions in which known people are reduced to an almost iconic simplicity, understood space restricted to an acutely limited rectangle. The summary in-tended by either abstraction is manifested by the way the dances are inserted in the films that contain them—as rever-ies or interludes or pauses—microcosms in the films' great for-ward narrative movements.

Dances appear throughout Ford's canon and have been thoroughly discussed elsewhere, but I want to concentrate on a few which have particular relevance to what I have to say here about community. Near the two-thirds point of *Fort Apache*, but clearly at that movie's center, stands the noncom-missioned officers' ball.[27] This is the most thoroughly realized of all Ford's dances; it is if anything a bit more completely composed than the film that contains it, a knotty problem pic-ture in Ford's canon.

This ball begins at the beginning—we see the musicians ar-rive—and ends at the end, the summarily announced last dance as Colonel Thursday breaks it up. We don't get to eat, but we know food is at the end of the room in the charge of Mrs. O'Rourke and Thursday's Mexican servant; we don't meet everybody but are introduced to many and know many of the rest already; we don't dance all the dances but we aren't forced to sit many out. This participation metaphor doesn't work too well, because this dance is formally distanced in comparison with the dance in *Clementine* or that of *They Were Expendable*, *Wagon Master*, *The Grapes of Wrath*, *Two Rode Together*, or *Drums Along the Mohawk*. In the sense that we are made to dance in *Two Rode Together* or *My Darling Clementine*, in *Fort Apache* we are only invited to watch. The camera moves in a way which choreographs the participants' dance, but our supposed participation with the dance is formally limited.

The three sergeants arrive almost as soon as the musicians and are subjected to breath inspection by O'Rourke. The dominant joke is drinking: their drinking or not drinking is linked to the dominant conceit of this segment of the film: best behavior and imitation of their betters. Best behavior and military discipline merge in the inspection, for it is a social inspection, as the underlying theme is class difference. Unlike what a Hitchcock film might make of this, class difference is here a central supporting member of the social structure. The officers arrive and are greeted by O'Rourke, and the tables turn as he, in command as the host, accepts from those normally his superiors, the guests, their necessary contribution of booze to spike the punch. It must not be spoken of in words, but only referred to by gesture. But the gesture has become so formalized a part of the arrival proceedings that it is a part of the expected ritual as well. O'Rourke seems embarrassed that the officers don't understand the ritual but must continue to gesture, and joke, persist in pointing out what they are doing. The ritual takes care of that. O'Rourke's advantage over Thursday may be a profound understanding of ritual.

There is a jump in the action, everyone now arrived and a dance just ending. The post's Doctor (Guy Kibbee) makes his way somewhat drunkenly (a link to the preceding installment) to the band platform to announce the Grand March. The inversion of roles is leveling. There is a sense in which officers and noncoms are equal tonight, but precedence holds: the colonel is announced (to join Mrs. O'Rourke), then Philadelphia Thursday (Shirley Temple), as the colonel's lady, is escorted by O'Rourke. In the carefully detailed sequence which brings us to the beginning of the Grand March, Ford gives us a pair of set-ups, one of which stresses the presence of the sergeants, the other of which omits them and stresses officers. As we go down the sequence of the bowing gentlemen and proffered arms and by-the-book escortings, we come to Mulcahy (Victor McLaglen) and Mrs. Collingwood (Anna Lee): propriety is stressed until Mulcahy meets and threatens Meacham the wicked proprietor of the trading post, and then must beg Mrs. Collingwood's pardon; and, as if propriety were all that held this evening in balance, his apology is accompanied visually by the almost magical clearing-up of confusion in their background as crowd becomes couple and couple in stately progression, leading to the central moment of the Grand March. The march itself is a beautifully edited sequence of a similar ordering balance. The column of twos is done in three angles (left to right; toward us, up right to down left; up left to down right) and then accelerated for the progress of fours and then eights (up right to down left and up left to down right; up right to down left and head-on). The merging is ritual, formal, majestic, and, one feels, as temporary as McLaglen's sobriety. But the idea that the Grand March ends the association between commission and noncommission is broken by Mrs. O'Rourke, who forces Thursday into the succeeding dance. Fonda's Thursday dances by the book, extremely well for a martinet (unlike his Lincoln in *Young Mr. Lincoln*, or his Earp in *Clementine*) and he seems happy to be dancing. Ford stresses the potential of balance here for a true merging of this community as he cuts from the Colonel and Mrs. O'Rourke, almost imperceptibly in midturn, to O'Rourke and Philadelphia. The dance ends and again there is a jump in time to the arrival of Captain York and Sergeant Beaufort (John Wayne and Pedro Armendariz) from their conclave with Cochise. The colonel looks up from his watch as he is checking the time, hears the report, immediately declares his intention to betray York's promise to Cochise, and asks that the ball be ended. In this sequence of shots Ford emphasizes again the distinctions between officers and noncoms. Alternately he holds out the possibility of a unity, a bridging of this gap in some common ideal. O'Rourke ends the ball, Beaufort falls on the punch table and is joined by the other sergeants, relieved now of the obligation of propriety (either by the Colonel's departure, the end of the ball, or some combination of these with the unhappiness at the Colonel's decision, which they know means some kind of hopeless action). They join in, Mulcahy lifting the punch bowl to drink from it. The last dance ("Good Night, Ladies") closes with Philadelphia Thursday and Lieutenant O'Rourke dancing and clinching on the porch.

This would be nothing more than a rather straightforward rendering of a simple series of actions were it not for its immediate juxtaposition with the assembly of the troops at dawn and the march out of the fort to meet Cochise. Ford takes the solemnity and formality of mounted men in formation, turning and parading, and sets that against the group of women who watch from some upper porch (not very firmly located geographically). The women are arrayed as a united force (we have glimpsed this before when they surrounded Phil Thursday as she returned from finding the massacred detachment), turning toward each other, or toward the troop in the kind of regular facing and not-facing, associating and not-associating, which have marked the bridging actions of the ball. But here against a melodramatic Ford sky their function has changed. They are without power, and almost before we have a chance to reflect on that, their unified group is broken by the arrival of the messenger with the news that Collingwood's orders have arrived: he can be called back from the hopeless mission. Mrs. Collingwood thinks about this only for a moment, and then affirms her powerlessness. She could do it, call him back, but this would violate her essence as military wife who, by definition, waits. She might well bring about the end of her husband's trust, and the image tells us this could be worse than the death it is becoming increasingly clear he must face. Marching is resumed.

This dance and its Grand March are the community, accepted standards, firm traditions, mutual dependency between officer and rank, the support of men by their women and their own certain strength, all abstracted to a dance of significance. That the dance's effort to bring unity and bridge divisions is always potential rather than actual, and that it represents peace and resolution in a problem movie of confusing dislocations and disjunctions, suggests one of the great frustrations of the immediate postwar period: confusing reality had returned, but the beautifully simplifying ideals would not just disappear. Or—conversely—the beautiful ideals were won, but confusing reality would not lie down and be vanquished by them.

Rehearsed this way with themes and meanings spelled out and described and noted, both ball and march seem pat; but I have suggested that this kind of retelling does violence. A Ford image rendered in expository prose is no longer a Ford image; Ford sequences cannot be fathomed by timing or system or diagram; they must be experienced and experienced again, felt in their leisure, at their time, with ease and suddenness, involvement and formal distancing felt just as he calculated them for us. In the two sequences I have traced, the distance in the first instance is like a dream of completeness: complete dance, incipient balance, summary representation, potential participation. In the troop's marching out it is like a fully realized pageant: the spectacle is not made inert by facelessness but brought to individualized force by the characters we spot carefully arrayed in systematic rank, by the others we know as they stand assembled as chorus, on that curiously placeless rampart he has chosen for the women. Choppiness and attenuated incident may make up the dominant pattern of the rest of *Fort Apache*, and this has perhaps brought us some of the repose and completeness of these sequences as they contrast to confusion, unassimilated loss, and misplaced ideals.

The massacre which must come will be followed by what looks like a poorly timed and overt appeal to the Long Blue Line, Wayne's face staring out through the reflection of the cavalry troop. It is poorly timed to what surrounds it in this movie, but is placed here in canonical relationship—a good relationship—to all the other stares through reflections in Ford—in *The Horse Soldiers*, *Cheyenne Autumn*, *The Grapes of Wrath*, *My Darling Clementine*. Here, in the parade, as we had earlier in the dance, we see the service's formal associations performing their functions without irony, as if function alone might give sufficient cause, these people and this place sufficient dignity even for a Custer's Last Stand.

The difference between this dance and the dance of the Sunday Morning Sequence of *My Darling Clementine* is a difference in the use of formal elements, how either is integrated in what surrounds it. Faulkner's statement that he drove nails to build a house, that they might make a pretty pattern afterwards but that that wasn't why he put them there, ought perhaps to be recalled here for Ford. Every formal element is not just an entry in some sort of sweepstakes for the Best Dance or the Best Parade or the Best Sergeant Anecdote contest: each is rather shaped to fit the particular corner (to cite another favorite Faulkner image) it was meant for. I think *Fort Apache*'s ball stands in the movie's middle as an attempt to bring some order to a disturbed and disturbing movie by some chance operation of its own very accomplished order. As if to emphasize this, Ford edits some of it to play under the titles. *My Darling Clementine*'s dance is part of an elegant gesture, the whole Sunday Morning Sequence, which is in its turn part of a confident and ordered movie. As in the escape sequence of *The Hurricane*, the dances expand beyond themselves into the rest of the movie, not only by virtue of the structure imposed by rhythm and editing, but by the nature of their abstracted microcosm: Earp's walk with Clementine, the parading of the cavalry troop become a part of either and thus become greater in combination with context.

If asked to list what is most "Fordian" about Ford movies, what does he steal from himself, almost everyone would, I think, list dances. I think our memory plays us a little false in this. There are not nearly so many dances in Ford films as our memory suggests, and there are far more dances in non-Ford Westerns than we may choose to remember. But as so often when memory betrays us, there's good reason. There is a dance (a rather energetic and abandoned one) in *The Great Train Robbery*, so it is as firmly placed as the chase in the heritage of movie and Western. Dances were a part of the narrative structure of action Westerns as Ford came to them. Lesser directors insert dances in Westerns (before they begin to imitate Ford) as scenes or transitions of narrative, or moments "apart" (see, for instance, the dance in the 1931 *Virginian*, not much more than a locus for the "swampy" baby-swapping by the cowboys). The detail of our memory plays us equally false: one remembers that Ford dances take place out of doors (*The Grapes of Wrath, Clementine, Hurricane*) and that many feature a Grand March (*Fort Apache*). But such details as well perhaps point to truth: space is always being altered, manipulated, and understood in a consistent formal concern, and perhaps the Grand March error suggests another of the consistent functions of dance in Ford: climactic community summary.

One could carry that too far, into an attempt to prove that Ford operates in a world ruled by rigorous ritual. Dances are the source of drama: before that they were among the earliest religious functions. They are a staple dramaturgical excuse in tragedy, pageant, grand opera, and ice-show spectacular alike.

But that point is off-center for my argument. Their incidence and their distinctive features are not as important as the freight Ford places on them and the formal care he lavishes upon them. They are formal, community, summary occasions. I think they all share a rather simple narrative function: a point of coming together, perhaps immediately preceding a more violent flying apart. The Halloween dance in *Drums Along the Mohawk* is not a very articulate Ford dance, but its function is carefully made: immediately after it Claudette Colbert follows Gil (Henry Fonda) as he returns to their house and eavesdrops on his private moment with his child. She then turns around and prays, "O God, if only this could go on and on forever." It cannot, of course, which is the point of the sequence, and her line makes us realize sharply what we probably knew before she said it: this quiet moment, almost a silent sequence by contrast with the noise of the dance, is a moment beyond the danger and struggle of these lives, as the dance is a moment removed, a moment of abstracted and concentrated meaning, as clearly inflected with visual and narrative force as any chase.

In the dance at Corregidor in *They Were Expendable*, John Wayne and Donna Reed in the hammock can for a moment pretend that they aren't there, that America is here in the hammock, that they are the folks back home—make, in other words, one archetype into another. But Robert Montgomery comes along to call off the dance as surely as Fonda's Colonel Thursday does in *Fort Apache*: by the book. Ford leaves Donna Reed in the swing, listening and not listening, but certainly realizing what is never said in words, that the value of the moment they just had is not doomed by what the men are now saying behind her at the end of the porch, but that their moment was doomed by its completeness: converted from a moment valued for its sameness to other moments, its similarity to the everyday of back home, into a moment which now must be valued as unique, the only moment apart. There is of course no dialogue to mark this recognition as there is in *Drums* (and perhaps this as well as anything marks the advance Ford has made in a few years in his own confident language), but in Donna Reed's eyes is carried as great a burden of Ford's visionary elegance as we saw there of suffering and exhaustion in the operating room.

In the first dance of *They Were Expendable* there isn't much dancing, but there is a kind of Grand March. The officers are hashing over events of the day which have led John Wayne's Rusty Ryan to a decision to request transfer. The noncommissioned officers and enlisted men, led again by Ward Bond, are at a separate and not equal celebration, but it is at their mustering-out party, Doc Charlie's (Jack Pennick's) retirement, that Ford signals us that we are about to see an exercise of variation on a theme: the radio behind the bar, in close-up, says, "We interrupt this program to bring you a special news bulletin . . ." and Ward Bond reaches over and turns it off. Probably the most frequently adduced convention of war pictures, or even pictures made during the war, was this ritual appeal to the stunning news bulletin of the Pearl Harbor attack, and Ford chooses to have it switched off.

The officers's dance is more gradually interrupted: an MP comes to the club manager, who in turn notifies the brass in descending order of rank, and once the important officers have risen and left, comes to the microphone to announce to the remainder that Pearl Harbor has been attacked. The officers and their ladies file out in the long-shot view Ford has established for us, craned above and at a three-quarters angle over their departing shoulders. As they file away a native singer steps to the microphone and begins to sing *My Country 'Tis of Thee* to the bizarre accompaniment of a Hawaiian guitar.

It is not that this sequence is touching or that it is based in a dangerously nostalgic sentiment (where were you when you heard about Pearl Harbor?), but that Ford so distances the event by means of the formal elements of understanding the place—angle, timing, and light and dark—and that he has in the rest of his canon so established for us the expectation for the pieces which he uses to form this jigsaw of meaning that he has given us the equipment to construct the sequence even before we see it. This or that more or less essential piece of the puzzle has been omitted. The stately march out replaces the Grand March: the last moment in the formal-dress whites, the last of the peacetime, bickering navy. The light-and-dark pattern omits almost all architectonic understanding of this space and in a sense we are once more out of doors, as in *The Grapes of Wrath* or the Sunday Morning Sequence. The rendition of the song by a foreigner is not an instance of Ford's much-touted jingoism but rather a measure of this woman's shock, extended to everyone there. She feels she should sing something, the band feels it can accompany, but it is a song as out of place here as the strains of *Red River Valley* which later back up our last look at the boatyard man (Russell Simpson) in the middle of the Philippine jungle. The passage becomes not so much recapitulation of stereotypical shock at the Pearl Harbor announcement as image for the coming-to-an-end of one set of assumptions and the beginning of a whole new set. Officers and their ladies will become a thing of the past because this news makes the Philippines the front lines; arguments about loyalty and transfers out, even the mustering-out of the chief petty officer, have been subsumed in a new form of community. Everything is changed utterly and our signal for this is, once again, a formal moment of completeness.

Even as *Seven Women* measures the distance Ford has come from *Stagecoach*, in this particular of the formal function of dance, *Two Rode Together* measures the distance Ford has moved after the war beyond the other dances. I have suggested that the repose and completeness of the dance in *Fort Apache* contrasts to the confusion and disruption which surround it in the rest of that movie. In *Two Rode Together* the film's climax in the lynching of Marty Powell's Indian-captive brother is woven into either end of the ball which marks the break McCabe (James Stewart) makes with the community which has hired him to bring back its children now made alien by another culture. At the dance community bands together in a perversion of its own supposed standards to reject both him and what he has brought back for them. The ball is no Grand March or completion or balanced bridging that the Ball in *Fort Apache* represents. Punch is served by Sergeant Posey (Andy Devine), the dances seem to come in sets with pauses in between, ranks mix it up, but what dominates is not the completeness or totality of the experience but rather the ladies' social rejection of Elena as a redskin's concubine and the resultant tripping-up of young officers, general disruption, and the talking-to with which McCabe and Gary (Richard Widmark) end the ball. Another ball ended, but this time not by the book. The shooting of all this (although much of the framing is beautifully balanced) concentrates on disruption. The editing makes the most of the disintegration of possible groups by reversals, sudden dislocation, and separation. Shooting, rhythm, and editing here are in formal patterns almost indistinguishable from the patterns Ford chooses to show us the Captive's killing of his supposed mother which precedes it and the lynching which follows the ball. If in *Fort Apache* Ford had chosen the rhythmic patterns of the massacre for the Grand March, we would have seen something like this.

Which is not to say that this ball is less formal. It is, in the sense that dislocation and reversal are less formal than are carefully arranged progressions and alternate symmetries. But this dislocation and disruption still depend on the distancing that made the ball of *Fort Apache* what it was. The difference is that community is no longer an ideal for potential good or depicted as a good in itself, but is, rather, the cause of this evil and precipitator of its inevitable hurt and carnage.

So we have moved from a dance (*Fort Apache*) which was a measure of ideal balance the community—and that movie—could not achieve, through dances (*Drums Along the Mohawk, They Were Expendable*) emblematic of the highest moments of achieved—but impossible to achieve again—bliss, to *Two Rode Together*. This final dance is not just arena for cruelty but instrument for its accomplishment. The ball—far from being a moment apart from the doubts and hazards of the post and the recovery of the captives—has become integrated in the downhill rush of disruptive events which light the community's way (as do those ever-present torches) to the lynching of its own son. Known is an irony here, and our knowing ranges from Sergeant Posey in the Jane Darwell mold to the Captive Boy who does not know himself (much less we him). He gains his place by escaping from one understood place of his cell (understood by us with him from the inside out) to achieve another understood place by embracing the tune of his infancy by grabbing for the music box seconds before he is dragged away to sudden death. Then McCabe can return home to find *his* understood space occupied by another's known face. What a different world is here. And what a different mode Ford has found to contain it.

The connection to Faulkner is obvious. Faulkner found poisonous community early and turned to benignant community later in the Trilogy; Ford did something like the opposite (even though we would be more accurate to acknowledge that darkness runs throughout both Faulkner and Ford). This formulation risks identifying a sense of community with a balance between optimism and pessimism. It is, of course, far more than that. It is that in Ford community may well be the subject and we find our relationship to what we see in how we participate in that community. In Faulkner, community may be atmosphere, environment, background, theme, allegory, philosophical matrix, subtext, but never subject. The concerns of Faulkner and Ford seem to touch or even to merge until we shift our critical emphasis from theme to means: the way Community and the Individual is manifested in the respective visions of these artists. Known people in an understood space is less appropriate to Faulkner than his own phrase of flesh-and-blood living people caught in the furious motion of being alive. For Ford the flesh-and-blood living people find the space they have been owed, the space of their essence, the place they've been headed for. This is not to say that time does not function in Ford, but that if we were to rate elements, time for Ford would come after space. For Faulkner it would come before. And for community this makes a difference, for these are two different kinds of realization: knowing this moment and finding this place; understanding what is past and how it put us there and knowing where we are and what surrounds us; ripeness and rightness. All these pairings can be applied to individual and community alike. Faulkner favors timing and Ford placement. And that is a profound difference in the very abstract worlds they have made for us and the very tangible ways in which we inhabit them.

FOUR

GENRE

In *A Song—for Anything* (No. 89 of *114 Songs*) Charles Ives set a disquisition on genre.[1] To the same straightforward tune he put three verses, one a love song, one a Yale song, one a hymn. The first repeat of the tune is, once we realize the words, wit; the second repeat is criticism, or perhaps theory. The tune should be played and sung as close to an exact repeat as the differing words allow because the whole (Ives would hold, the *only*) value of the song is the exercise, the comment, the trick. To vary the performance in order to accommodate the different subjects or programs for each of the three "songs" would be to undercut the point of the whole. The tune does for each what it has just done for the one before and what it is about to do again for the one after.

The repeats, with varying words, assert an essential generic truth: if Ives's devising has been right and the repetition careful, the notes of the song will tug exactly the same strings in each cause—and, the song tells us, in whatever cause. This first assertion is a cynical truth: song as manipulator, tune as automaton. But to make it work, Ives has had to believe for a moment in what he is doing each of three times, or the words would ring as empty; more important, the song continues to do his believing for him. Early on in working with Ives we learn to deal with apparent self-contradictons like this one, but we also learn quickly to rein in our tendency to think him always and only ironic and satirical. He is rather infrequently so. He really means it about America, about God, parenthood, war, about independence and self, about Emerson and Hawthorne and the Alcotts. It would be a mistake to think that he means it about God and Yale *as* this song means it, but it would be an equal mistake to transfer to him our desire to make *America Variations* into a joke about America instead of taking its greater (and proper) point, its comment upon music. To do so would be unjust to the piece and to Ives. Or to think, God forbid, that he means in *A Song—for Anything* to send up Yale, God, or love.

Of course, Ives thrice denies *A Song—for Anything*. In a note at the end of *114 Songs* he writes:

Nos. 28, 53, 85, 86, 87, 89, 90, 96, have little or no musical value—a statement which does not mean to imply that the others have any too much of it). These are inserted principally because in the writer's opinion they are good illustrations of types of songs, the fewer of which are composed, published, sold or sung, the better it is for the progress of music generally. It is asked—probably a super-fluous request—that they not be sung, at least in public, or given to students except as examples of what not to sing.[2]

He adds a note at the foot of the score:

NOTE: —The song above is a common illustration (and not the only one in this book) of how inferior music is inclined to follow inferior words and "vice-versa." The music was originally written to the sa-cred words printed last, (and the best of the three.) Some thirty years ago it was sung in a country church and even as a response after the prayer. The congregation not only tolerated it, but accepted it apparently with satisfaction. That music of this character is less fre-quently heard in relegious [sic] services now-a-days is one of the signs of the wholesome progress of music in this country. An "Amen" was tacked on the end of this song; a relative of the composer remarked, at the time, that it was about as appropriate to this kind of a tune as a benediction would be after an exhibition of the "Circassian Beauty" at the "Danbury Fair."[3]

His third disclaimer is found in his listing of the song as one of "Nos. 85 to 92, 'Sentimental Ballads.'"

But to deny that the song is music worth serious considera-tion (or even worth singing) is not to deny that it has any-thing to say about music or to deny the song's efficacy as criti-cal act or as musical gesture. Each of the three "songs" of No. 89 is clearly a song Ives is less proud of *as music* than *Cir-cus Band* (No. 56) or *Slow March* (No. 114), but all are clearly a part of *114 Songs'* musical statement, a part of the main: "All that is left is out on the clothes line,—but it's good for a man's vanity to have the neighbors see him—on the clothes line." I think such "disclaimed" songs partake most seriously—certainly more seriously than do some of the *europäischen* art songs—of the larger philosophical thesis of 114 *Songs*, of the songs' critical and theoretical statement. Without assertions of negative value Ives's prose would not be characteristic; without such negative songs neither would 114 *Songs*. He meant to publish everything here ("I have merely cleaned house") as certainly as he meant to write it all.

A song has a *few* rights the same as other ordinary citizens. . . . If it wants to beat around in the valley, to throw stones up the pyramids, or to sleep in the park, should it not have some immunity from a Nemesis, a Rameses, or a policeman? Should it not have a chance to sing to itself, if it can sing? to enjoy itself, without making a bow, if it can't make a bow? . . . If it happens to feel like trying to fly where humans cannot fly,—to sing what cannot be sung—to walk in a cave, on all fours,—or to tighten up its girth in blind hope and faith, and try to scale mountains that are not—Who shall stop it!

—In short, must a song
always be a song![4]

I think the sum total of this complex "Postface" and its reflexive and mercurial persona and voice is that in it Ives says, What I have written I have written—all of it. And it's not there to demonstrate how good I am at music. Let me prove it. He has published this hunk of music, 114 *Songs*. To this music he has set an afterword, the "Postface," as reflexive and self-denying as any of the songs, to act as credo, introduction and structuring (as Tom Wolfe says, "Without a theoretical statement to go with it, a work of art cannot exist"[5]), but no theoretical statement, no matter how ambivalent, can claim to say what any one of these songs can (what words alone could so claim?). Ives chooses an oblique and sometimes self-abnegating persona to sing his creed, and this is the voice that hovers over this hunk of music.

He means to answer one bit of his own self-questioning catechism:

A man never knows his vices and virtues until that great and solemn event, that first sunny day in spring when he wants to go fishing, but stays home and *helps* his wife clean house. . . . Wedged in between the sewing machine and the future he examines himself, as every man in his position should do;—'What has brought me to this?—Where am I? Why do I do this?' These are natural inquiries. They have assailed thousands before our day; they will afflict thousands in years to come and probably there is no form of interrogation so loaded with subtle torture—unless it is to be asked for a light in a strange depot by a man you've just selected out of seventeen thousand as the one man the most likely to have a match. Various authors have various reasons for bringing out a book, and this reason may or may not be the reason they give to the world; I know not and care not.[6]

The songs intractably refuse to address a much more superficial question: "It stands now [the printing of this collection], if it stands for anything, as a kind of 'buffer state,'—an opportunity for evading a question, somewhat embarrassing to answer,—'Why do you write so much——, which no one ever sees?' There are several good reasons, none of which are worth recording."[7] The songs of 114 *Songs* stand as an approach by Ives to the prime question of identity: Ives sees identity to be a man's purpose, his seriousness, what he thinks it is that counts about him: "This is a question which a man must answer for himself. It depends to a great extent, on what a man nails up on his dashboard as 'valuable.'"[8] One thing Ives nailed to his dashboard was that the most advanced and basic truths are those which are the most accessible: "To see the sunrise a man has but to get up early, and he can always have Bach in his pocket."[9] Clothesline, dashboard, scraps and bits.

It is not for me to judge the world unless I am elected. It is a matter which lies between the composer and his own conscience, and I know of no place where it is less likely to be crowded. . . . Some have written a book for money: I have not. Some for fame; I have not. Some for love; I have not. Some for kindlings; I have not. I have not written a book for any of these reasons or for all of them

together. In fact, gentle borrower, I have not written a book at all—
I have merely cleaned house.[10]

A *Song—for Anything* is a speck, or maybe three specks, of
this sweeping-out. And of that disquisition on genre as well.
The disquisition does not say everything Ives has to say on
genre, because he spent his career exploring genre even as he
explored form and content, statement and theory, solo and ensemble, heard and unheard. In particular he spent the length
of 114 *Songs* exploring genre. This universe of songs was
grouped in an essentially generic system: "Songs of War" (49–
50), "Songs based on hymn-tune themes" (44–47), "Street
Songs" (52–56), "Sentimental ballads" (85–92), as well as
"German songs" and "French songs."

Genre is not just a listing by type: it's the backbone of
American art. I think genre is two things: it's the type of thing
a lot of people do so it is popular in its origins, in its inten-
tions, and frequently in its results. Genre is a system of heritage, by which one work of art can inherit what has been done
in that art (or in other arts) before it came along. This makes
genre of considerable significance to first-rate artists: genre
plays a mediational role—especially for American artists,
feeling their way for a thing to be that's independent of that
European Older Brother. Genre connects a work of art to
what is, or what has been, or may still be going to be, popular.
When Graham Greene writes his "entertainments" he does
not stop being a first-rate novelist (some would say he is even
better at this than he is at his mainstream novels). Beetho-
ven's dances, Howard Hawks's Westerns are no less art because they have touched base with genres or spring from them,
and these pieces can be judged in comparison with other
pieces from those genres. But neither Greene's "entertainments" nor Hawks's Westerns are made by the genres or even
accomplished within them. C. S. Lewis uses science fiction
and is claimed by that literary ghetto as one of its saints, but to
see what he is doing in the *Perelandra* series as being no more

than science fiction would be as foolish as it would be to claim it was *other than* s-f. Alan Ayckbourn and Tom Stoppard use British and American sitcom. And so does Joe Orton.

Genre is more necessary to an understanding of American art than it is for the art of any other nation. American art depends so on genre, I think because of that Little Brother complex, the uncertainty of national identity. American is national only in an allegorical sense because America is a compound, a melted potful of many nationalities, an invented persona. Emerson calls upon Americans to invent themselves and they obligingly try to do so even though they seem a little surprised that they need to (*they* know who they are). But in order to do so they borrow from wherever they can, character-istics and gestures from which they compound (as Dr. Fran-kenstein cobbles up his monster) this new thing.

Maybe it's because art has always offended Americans by being of so little *use*, maybe it's a part of our national embar-rassment at anything intellectual or a part of that hangdog at-titude American artists seem to have to adopt. Maybe it's be-cause we have to make (in Norman Mailer's terms) boxers of our artists, competing with each other for the Big Prize of the Great American Novel or the Best Painter of His Generation, that our artists in their defense come so to depend on genre. It's a stopgap common identity which can stand in for them until they settle on an identity of their own.

But depend they do. In *A Song—for Anything* Ives means to include many of these senses of genre. The types listing at the head of *114 Songs* says something to him of divergent intent, of audience, shape, and tone. To sing a hymn is not to sing *Yankee Doodle*, and that *not* touches on singer, song, and hearer, Ives tries always to be conscious of both negative and positive boundaries of genre—that is, what makes a hymn a hymn and what it could contain which would make it not a hymn. When a tune stretches itself over three divergent sets of lyrics the thing to notice is not so much that the distinction between one and the other genre is insignificant, but that each of the three genres still works in tandem even though no note of the tune has changed. This is some kind of enforcement of the power genre can wield, not a diminution of that power.

Genre is one thing Ives has nailed to his dashboard. He knows that much of genre is machine and although he seems to have nothing much but contempt for that kind of machine, he knows at the same time that this is not to say that genre is formula. It is not. But it is a device to take over certain artistic functions so that certain other functions are freed to attain a more advanced level of abstraction, variation, or elaboration. When we hear the Yale song of A Song—for Anything we listen to its sappy sentiment for a personified institution and forget for a moment how silly it is to sing a loving song to a set of educational structures. The tune has taken over—such songs are sung—and suspended for us our disbelief. To sing to Yale is possible because this song is a Yale song. This is a simple example. Faulkner's horror story Sanctuary freed him, he said, to use the tool of "sensationalism" and avoid some of the responsibilities of rounded character, presentable event, believable setting. Some of Two Rode Together's automatic Westernness (the Marshal, the fancy lady who owns the town, the wagon train, the cavalry) enables the movie's extreme abstraction, its shortcuts which make it so distinctive (the scene in the teepee, McCabe's drunken and bitter diatribe, the killing of Stone Calf, the violence of the lynching).

When an artist gives himself over to genre he is either a supremely confident artist who knows what he is doing (as all of these are) or a fledgling who comes to genre to get all the help he can get. Middling artists hate genre because it shows them up either as pikers compared to Ford or Ives—in other words, as aging fledglings—or as failures (premature greats). But if an artist wants to be ordinarily competent or commonly great, genre is just the ticket, because what is for one a road map is for the other a launching pad. This metaphor seems out of control, but genres are extreme and so extreme metaphor is appropriate. Genre is the land of extremes. Unless one surrenders to its mastery as Ford does in *My Darling Clementine* or *Wagon Master* or Ives does in *He Is There!* or Faulkner in "Elly," genre is not possible; cheating, or cuteness or send-up (*Raise the Titanic, Return of the Jedi, The Loved One*) are the death of genre (as is so frequently seen in the historical decay characteristic of the late stages in the evolution of genre); variation, evolution, and compromise are its life. Repetition is at its heart.

Faulkner, Ford, and Ives were all masters of genre and each had an inspired respect for different of its gifts. I believe Faulkner's realization of its values came late, after a lot of early experiment and sometimes halfhearted or apologetic use of genre support. I think maybe he distrusted genre for a time as too popular to be any good to him. Ford and Ives never for a moment seem to have doubted that genre was as much the stuff of art as structure or engagement or shape was. But they never doubted this in different ways: *The Lost Patrol* is as certain of its generic basis as *Liberty Valance* is and it has much less genre to go on, early as it is. *Slow March* is a sad parlor song in a different relationship to its generic basis. Each artist came to his realization by a different path—Ives by knowing that his father was a musician although "only" a bandmaster, Ford not quite from the cradle but certainly from the time of his apprenticeship as he learned the strange nature of the art he worked (which called itself an industry; which claimed, but didn't even believe, it was an art). Faulkner got part of his later sense of the dignity of genre from that same art of the movies—the generic input of movies is significant to the Gangster-picture elements of *Sanctuary* and to the Southern-picture antebellum scenes of *Absalom, Absalom!*—but Faulkner was always less committed to the legitimacy of genre as an artistic function than Ford and Ives.

For the genres Ives has to work with, *A Song—for Anything* provides a more or less representative sample. If we imagine that the Yale song is akin to patriotic song and the love song

akin to ballad, there would be lacking only the art song or parlor piece and the formal European *lieder* to complete Ives's survey here of the available genres in 114 *Songs*. Aside from the
influence of the French and German lyrics on the settings' musical manners and modes, these genres form the backbone of
114 *Songs*. There is in addition the generic complication of
quotation and allusion—to popular song, hymn, anthem—
which runs throughout Ives's larger pieces.

I think it is fair in general to say that Ives took the cue for
his music from the words—this sequence is significant when it
comes to genre, because words and music can represent two
different genres, but once this is said it is also fair to add that
the words do not dominate the songs: the balance between
singer and "accompaniment" is one of the most significant
characteristics of the Ives song. Of any song it could be said
that the accompaniment is a vital part, but one has not heard
an Ives song when one has heard only singer or only piano (or
only knows the song in one of the gussied-up "arrangements"
by other hands for orchestra and chorus). The space that
singer and piano share or that they create between them manifests a significant alteration to either, and it is this space we
find ourselves listening to: think of *He Is There!* (50), *Slow
March* (114), *Serenity* (42), *The Side-Show* (32), or *The Indians*
(14). The question of singer and piano in Ives's songs is akin
to the function of words and images in a somewhat word-
dominated Ford picture like *The Man Who Shot Liberty Valance*. There it would be a mistake to depend on the words of
dialogue for one's final sense of what is happening or of what it
means, but the images are there less capable than elsewhere in
Ford's films of going it alone with the soundtrack turned off.

In addition to larger genre in Ives, there is also the matter
of generic manner. I could designate four or five "manners" of
the Ives song—something less than formal outline, something
more than stylistic tic—into which Ives songs fall: imitation
Lieder, art song, antique ditty, rhythmic game. These are
rather rough-and-ready categories but they make for me a

rather significant footnote to Ives's use of genre, correspond to
something I always hear in the songs, and perhaps correspond
to something we might call the genres of the Ivesian. I think
the balance of these elements of manner, genre, form, and
text determine the curiously backward-looking experiment
which *114 Songs* represents and it is this I'm trying to get at.

Beyond A *Song—for Anything* and its disquisition on genre,
Ives's practice in genre is remarkably straightforward—even
cautious. One can think of genre as a recipe: How many of
these things does it take to make a Western? How many things
can I leave out and still have an art song? Does it matter if
I put the eggs or shortening in first? Or one can treat genre as
a set of mixed spare parts—chase, recognition, stripping of
military rank, even cockroach race—all these are elements of
film genre movable from Musical to Western to Spy. Compared to Faulkner's piecemeal mixed-media approach to generic recipe, to say nothing of Ford's free manipulation of
genre—one genre layered on another top of another, freely
put in with a loaded brush, as it were—Ives's use of genre is
rather simple. In *He is There!* Ives isolates generic elements of
a variety of warlike patriotic songs. He seems to be intent (almost like Stravinsky searching Bellini's operas for the essence
of melody) on locating within these the source of the songs'
force and energy. He finds it in breathless openings, in rous-
ing closings and then in one of his most nervous combinative
strokes, connects some openings and some closings by means
of some oddball joints. The result is a song with narrative but
without what one might expect in narrative development. The
lyrics for two stanzas seem to be a straightforward and simple
tale of one lad on either side of the Great War. The third is an
exordium to the worth of the fervor the first two have narrated. But the music runs counter to narrative *and* exhortative
force and it combines with snatches of other such songs to become the burden of the song's energy. The result is itself a
wonderful patriotic song which even as it thrills in the man-

ner of such songs shows up the devices of that genre without undercutting or compromising the end and aim of the song.

At the River (45) is a hymn to a hymn. Ives is content to use up a song just demonstrating that it was written right to begin with: he makes a few simple alterations to an old favorite and these few changes have made all the difference. The challenge match he sets up for himself is to retain the immediate accessibility the original hymn so brilliantly displays (the original is one of Ford's favorite musical set pieces both in his movies and played as mood music on the sound stage) and then to enhance it with a simplicity cognate to the original. Ives accomplishes all this with such skill that once we are familiar with it, *his* tune can spring to mind before the original. It's right, seems at home, strikes us almost as better. Ives is rehearsing genre and performing an exercise within the bounds of that genre's rules—indeed, within the bounds of an existing song: to make something new, simple enough that it could have had truly common or popular origins, which attempts to replace the genuine article, the original song's tune, with his new one. He succeeds miraculously.

Faulkner in rehearsing a ghost story in "A Rose for Emily" attempts something of the same thing. He takes elements of Miss Havisham from Dickens's *Great Expectations* and attempts to replace that powerful archetype in our minds with a new archetype more sinister, more malignant, more affectingly pitiable. He succeeds so well that we cannot, having once seen Emily Grierson, see Miss Havisham without transferring to her a hint of Emily's necrophiliac standard. But Faulkner, like Ives, has gone beyond this. He has suggested that the recluse was recluded by us (are not we now a part of that "we of the town" the story so cunningly assumes?) and this gives our involvement in the finding of that single iron-gray hair, and our guilt in breaking down the door to find it a peculiarly tangible force.

General William Booth (not one of *114 Songs*), surely the most powerful of all American songs, is a different sort of generic expression, one that brings up a great many new issues. Ives, by combining all his manners—of *Lieder, Sturm und Drang*, art song, patriotic, hymn tune, love song, and mob chorus—in a combination-of-ingredients product, moves *General Booth* beyond the normal boundaries of song into chorale, drama, operatic ensemble, tone poem. It again is interested in both positive and negative boundaries of the song and keeps tempting us to break down with it another generic or media boundary to describe one or another of its so effective extremes as if that extreme were just the mainline for a song. The musical and combinative extremes are so persuasive that *General William Booth* demands an almost severe performance because anything more seems hammy or melodramatic: the song has done so much of its own singing that to "perform" it beyond that severe measure seems to defy its straighforward self, not so much gilding the lily as rowing the hovercraft.

All of these songs and their generic involvements raise one particular and difficult matter again and again: Ives's use of the tunes of others, his quotations, *hommages*, use of snatches of melodies of the songs of others. Elliot Carter, in an interview in Perlis's *Charles Ives Remembered* (p. 145), says he regrets this habit as an element which restricted Ives's invention ("have no artistic pretensions and reveal little fundamental musical imagination"), became a governor on the speed and reach of his genius. Nothing could be farther from the truth. The Carter statement assumes that Ives resorts to these snatches as the lyricist of a popular song (Oscar Hammerstein II, for instance) might resort to a dummy tune, in order to give his music some unearned incremental advantage, a phony to work with to make up for a lack of substantial material of his own at the time. Even when the use of the tune material is exhaustive (as in the use of *What a Friend We Have in Jesus* in the second movement of the *First Piano Sonata*) Ives is not substituting this material for a lack of his own but rather attempting to find within borrowed and quoted stuff the completion of the potential his modes, manners, and manipulations can find within the borrowed. When (as in *He Is There!*) quotation is rife and various there is a different impact. Ives expects the quotations either to bring along with them some of the emotional, the generic, or the narrative freight from the original, or to ring like an echo, bring with them some barely remembered import from some disused corridor of our minds as we listen, something like those partial notes he works into the symphonies, or his lost trombones, swallowed up by the surrounding sounds of the orchestra, things that hover in the score on the edge of the unheard in the world. Or he changes the nature of the originals by slicing them up, putting them into combinations which alter the generic content of the originals, combining them with other snatches of other glees and by laying them end to end, he shows the new life available to the segmented tune when it has been put into a new context.

This, of course, corresponds to a model familiar to students of genre. When in *They Were Expendable* John Ford puts a boatyard in the middle of the Philippine jungle he perches on its front steps an owner Russell Simpson, the fiddle-playing Elder of *My Darling Clementine* and familiar to many other Ford landscapes. He gives him a "kag" of whiskey, puts a shotgun across his knees, and plays the *Red River Valley* on the soundtrack. What has brought all this to the heart of darkness but genre, generic quotation, generic cross-reference, whistling of old tunes on the porch in the dark? Faulkner's use of the conventions of the lynching story in "Dry September" and *Light in August* is a different kind of example.

I've written in *Faulkner's Narrative* about Faulkner's use of genre in *Sanctuary* and *Light in August* and various of the short stories. I would reassert most of those earlier positions, but I think I might be a little fuller now about how genre works. I suggested then some of the small manners of generic input, ranging from those that can give a story its whole shape (as in those uses of the "lynching story") to those that impart shape or flavor for only a part (as in the cracker-barrel manner of *The Hamlet*) or provide narrative shape (as in the little boy who knew too much of "That Will Be Fine," "Two Soldiers," "Shingles for the Lord"). But beyond these there are some more considerable manners—for Faulkner the great manners of the Southern gothic and the genre of Southernness, the second most significant regionalism (next to the Western) in American generic art. In Faulkner this becomes nearly a geography or a sociology: Joanna Burden's murder in *Light in August*, bits of the tonal quality and the trappings of Quentin's and Shreve's antebellum inventions at Harvard upon the distant Sutpen for *Absalom, Absalom!*, all of "A Rose for Emily," and most everything about the latter-day Southern-gothic manner of the Memphis of *Sanctuary*. There is the great literary structure of historical romance (the anchovy raid in *Flags in the Dust* and *Sartoris*, the odor-of-verbena segment of *The Unvanquished*, the substance of Hightower's visions in *Light in August*). Both Southern gothic and historical romance are accepted genres, and I do not mean to suggest by alluding to them that Faulkner writes *within* them. Genre in the hands of genius is just not like that. Faulkner uses elements, clues, trappings, settings drawn from them to figure their landscapes, to inform the actions of his characters, even (at least in the case of the anchovy raid) to fashion a shape, but none of the books or stories produced by these great manners is *within* that genre or even an instance of that genre. I think this is true because of that difficult characteristic of genre I've already mentioned: geniuses are attracted to genres and thrive in their midst yet are not formed by them. Had *Absalom, Absalom!* been the work of a hack it could have fallen within genre fiction. But as Faulkner wrote it, it only depends upon the great manner but does not fall within it. Faulkner tends to employ genres in units shorter than his wholes, then runs them through a variety of exercises sequentially. Genre for him becomes a series of costumes or disguises, a way of getting free of his subject's restrictions by shifting some of the burdens of authorship, tone, and style into an overdrive of these genres of choice.

Rather than falling within a genre the master makes his own, Faulkner what we call the Faulknerian, Ford the Fordian, Ives what is Ivesian. Elements drawn from quite conventional prototypes, models, and predecessors may be quite at home in such a "master genre," but one could never confuse the Fordian use of Western or romantic or immigrant elements with anyone else's use of Western or romantic or immigrant elements. In the Ivesian song and the Fordian moment, mixture can frequently be the mode, but it's not the only mode. Ives can expand genre by artful combination of ingredients (*General William Booth*), Faulkner by stylistic manners (in *Light in August*), Ford by genre combination (*The Wings of Eagles*). Master genres try the borders of conventional genres by discovering that they are capable of including much that the genres never had the sense to get invented for themselves: Ives pushing the heard to the edges of the unheard (the *Third* and *Fourth Symphonies*), Faulkner working the high seriousness of melodrama to the edge of tragedy (*Light in August, Absalom, Absalom!*), Ford finding new recipes by reducing even further the minimum requirements for a genre (*Wagon Master, Three Godfathers*). Or innovative and rehabilitative rehearsal and exercise within the bounds of genre (*Wagon Master, At the River*, "Dry September").

Ford is, of course, more difficult, because film genre is a more difficult and busier category than that for song or story, and he provides a puzzling nest of problems certainly not soluble in short compass. Ford is best known for the Western, and it's possible to mistake this one genre for his best work: the temptation for critics is to make everything he does a modified Western (*The Lost Patrol, Mogambo, Drums Along the Mohawk, The Horse Soldiers*), even if it might be more truly representative of his work as a whole, as well as being more just to the work at hand, to call even his Westerns extensions of his early efforts in the domestic frontier, or rural Americana, the story of the American family (as all of this appears, for instance, in *The Searchers*, or in *Three Godfathers*).

Second, Ford is the forgotten author of a major film genre, the empire film, in *Black Watch* (1929), *The Lost Patrol* (1935), and *Wee Willie Winkie* (1939).[11] He might have been aiming for something else, but this is what he made.

Third, Ford never quite seems to hit the mark when he uses generic landmarks (the political background of James Stewart in *Liberty Valance*, Andy Devine's character function in that film and others, Mae Marsh as white captive in *Two Rode Together*). This, of course, is the continual state of *auteurs*: beginners and hacks make a neater and falser history of genres.

Fourth, Ford so expands the potential of a given genre that his work can *seem* inattentive to the norms and measures of that genre as seen in the work of others: *Wagon Master* sails right past beginning movie watchers if they are still counting the cactuses or looking for a hero in a pale hat—or, indeed, looking for a hero at all.

Fifth, and again a paradox, some of his films are the most straightforward examples of genre (*Stagecoach*), some are the most difficult-to-understand of that particular genre (*Seven Women, The Wings of Eagles*). Let us take up first that missing of the mark, perhaps even take this issue to represent the problems of all the others, because it may finally be the simplest. When we consider that most of the pictures Ford made were set in the past it is surprising that so few come out to be characteristically (or even definitively) Costume Pictures. One of the problems with Costume, unique to this genre, is that of somewhat less than riveting subject matter and emotional involvement. Costume is a most powerful force: the least hint of it can destroy the Western-ness of a Western. Take *Wagon Master* as Ford's genre-setting and style-setting Western. Surely a batch of Mormons is a secure anchor for a Costume Picture, or at least for strong Costume elements: they settled in the West in a period certainly fixed, they looked such-and-such a

way and had such-and-such hallmarks. But by the time Ford
has finished with them they have been so integrated with the
medicine show, the outlaw family, the squaw dance, and those
Indians that we could swear that Mormons, like the rocks of
Monument Valley, were an auteurist signature rather than
representations of factual historic beings. *The Informer* is perhaps a Costume Picture, but although I am never eager to defend either its virtues as a good movie or its characteristic
Ford-ness, it seems successfully to have translated the Black
and Tan into a never-never-land army, more akin to the Nazi
Gestapo, which would come so to dominate our generic consciousness in the next few years to follow than to anything
of Ireland—never-never of time and almost of place. Ford's
Ireland, between *The Informer* and *The Quiet Man* (and off
screen the Ireland we have inferred as background for the
rakehell cavalry sergeants of *Rio Grande*, *Fort Apache*, *She
Wore a Yellow Ribbon*, and others, and the crew of *The Long
Voyage Home*), seems to be a geographic constant, but so
much a dream (in comparison with Ford's America) as to lack
a world beyond the details of nationality which Ford selects to
represent its complete sociology (see the chosen professions
displayed, for instance—part genre, but part pure Ford). No-
time costuming (in which the designer seeks to obscure specific period details) is at one with that favorite anecdote of
Ford's vision of Cochise on the hill with his pipe ("but he isn't
smoking any cigarette") may be taken as an exemplary account of how the Costume elements probably bit the dust one
by one as a Ford picture progressed through its shooting. He
preferred myth to authenticity. No-Time Setting or Non-
specific Past would be a fair description not only of *The Quiet
Man* but of *The Hurricane* and quite a bit of *The Grapes of
Wrath*, *How Green Was My Valley*. *The Wings of Eagles*, a great
movie but a problem movie in almost every way, conceives for
itself a specific function for this Non-specific Past, manifests an
approach to the uses of nostalgia and the failure of sea stories
out of that past to sustain the characters through what has

proved to be a difficult present. Ford smears stuff on the lens, Technicolors up the reminiscence, does everything but introduce cute title cards to antique the Teens and Twenties derring-do of Mr. and Mrs. Spig Wead, but except for the automobile (more Chitty-Chitty-Bang-Bang than sure temporal anchor), the movie never goes to the point of a Costume Picture, to show us how it was then, for that is not to its point. Rather Ford here concentrates on how this past fails to be relevant to the movie's present even when we have sat there watching the past when it was still present to us in the picture. None of this will mend Spig's back or cure his wife's drinking problem. The picture will not become *now* because in part it is never very firmly *then*. The way Ford uses it in the movie just makes this past *other*.

Fort Apache (the "ambulance" of the opening), *Rio Grande* (old-fashioned clothes-washing), *She Wore a Yellow Ribbon* (the operation in the wagon in mid–cavalry march), *The Fugitive* (those anticlerical Mexicans) all introduce firm factual historical Costume elements, but then they manage to understate them or render them into digressions, so that each of these elements finally becomes no more important than the constant reminders of Non-specific Oldness that pepper an average historically oriented Western. *Cheyenne Autumn* and *The Horse Soldiers* are probably Costume Pictures (certainly if we want to claim that the latter is the greatest movie of the Civil War it might be convenient to think they were). Neither, probably, is dominated by sure elements of Western. But *The Horse Soldiers*, despite its history-book introduction (complete with maps) aboard U. S. Grant's Mississippi steamboat, its Brady photographs taken in the cavalry camp, its real-monument plantation and plantation belle, never really becomes a slave of conventional antebellum (or rather bellum) Costume elements of the romance of the Old South. Considering it's a Costume Picture, it's rather odd that it's not a Southern picture.

I think the most nearly perfect movie I know is the military-school segment of *The Horse Soldiers*.[12] The portrait of Jefferson behind the desk of the priestly headmaster, the foreign legion hats of the cadets are certainly Costume elements in that beautiful inserted movie-within-a-movie, but the movie as a whole as surely avoids the generic hallmarks and the specifics of the genre, in part by avoiding the characteristic wordiness of the Costume Picture, the telling us over and over again ("That's Bleriot flying the Channel") which the Costume Picture finds so necessary to its identity (is Costume, after Whodunit, the second-most-talky genre?). This by contrast does everything it does with as few words as possible.

How does Ford do it? Elsewhere I have suggested as the characteristic hallmark of the Costume Picture the quill pen, taking my cue from the studio executive who didn't want no more of them pictures where guys write with feathers.[13] Recall the scene in *The Horse Soldiers* in the raided Newton Station as John Wayne's Colonel Marlowe, drinking in reaction to the death of one of his soldiers (which he blames on the medical profession), has an exchange with Constance Towers which seems very nearly the essence of the movie. Behind them during this conversation is a wood stove with a fancy heat-recovering stovepipe, quill pen among heating devices if there ever was one, as telltale a Costume signal (in the midst of this very twentieth-century exchange) as the patio salad set and barbecue pit of *The Egyptian* or *Samson and Delilah*. But still Costume fails to take over the picture, because character and the Fordian—a greater cause and a greater generic manner—will not permit it to. Our knowledge of the Costume Picture informs this argument about war in the bar, it informs the period warfare which not only speaks to pastness but is perhaps the most telling visual description of punitive materiel raids and Civil War patrol action on film, certainly beyond anything in Griffith. The movie through all this resolutely resists becoming a Costume Picture.

But contrast Ford's triumph over a consuming genre by thinking of Cecil B. De Mille's happy surrender. His Westerns

(*The Plainsman, Western Union*) are Costume Pictures, and his Costume (*Samson and Delilah, The Ten Commandments, The Unconquered*) are *echt* Costume. In *The Sign of the Cross* an authentic ram's-head cup appears and the movie stops: it's like the Griffith title card in *Intolerance* about the Babylonians' development of tiled bricks, announcing the historical *effort* at the expense of whatever subliminal re-creation the movie as a whole might have been trying to build up.[14] This is not meant as an invidious comparison of the two directors: to stack De Mille up against Ford is not a meaningful critical act (and not even much fun).

I think the manners of individual directors tell us something significant of the shape of genre as a whole, in something of the same way that the subgenres of horror—wolfman, monster, mad doctor—are more significant to that genre than are its more general hallmarks. Moving in the opposite direction, we can find that genre in general can tell us something about the measures of genius.

So what can be made of these three together, these artists working sometimes similar veins of the genres of divergent arts? That genre is closer to the surface of art in America than in Europe. That as a result our popular culture comes closer to our high culture at the point of intersection where genius meets genre. That these connections represent for each artist some kind of separate peace with those dangers which the act of engaging with a genre brings with it (as the terms "genre music," "genre painting," "genre fiction" suggest). And that each individual solution—separate peace, accommodation, manner—says something not just about the genre he engages in, but about the artist himself.

I suppose the most important thing about all this is a confirmation of something I've already said: engaging with genre is not a sign of weakness for these artists but a sign of strength. When Faulkner finally gets back around to his "Boys' Book" after *The Unvanquished, The Reivers* is not only a peculiar instance of that genre but Faulkner has worked it in such a way that it becomes a very odd form of anti-action, reversing what the Boys' Book must ultimately depend upon, direct action directly narrated. Ives's most moving song, *Slow March*, is an elegy—for a dog. Ford finds his generic end in *Seven Women*; the supreme artist of men and women out of doors finds himself locked in a Chinese missionary compound, but he is still no less the original—and the most personal—master the cinema has yet found. What odd works result from such conventional engagements.

EPILOGUE

AGAINST THE GRAIN

Phineas Barnum's traveling companion that day in England made a stab at replicating his Yankee speech by quoting him saying, "We've none of them old fixings in Amerikey." *Amerikey* (and I doubt the word sounded that way to any but British ears) would be a good term for America as described by Barnum's tone of world-beating brag: we did it before and we can do it again, Tom Thumb shown on the same street with Shakespeare (*in person*) and beating him all hollow. The ambivalent counterpart for this is the dark side of our land, what we hear all the time called '*Murka*, the chthonic world of the American unconscious Raoul Walsh's films so tellingly depict and Richard Slotkin's literary history describes: the Indians, the witch-hunters, lynchings, My Lais, rapes, and mutilations.[1] In this world of multiple ambivalence, of course, to pin down something like this is like standing on a bushel of eels. Barnum speaks from Amerikey. But "There's one born every minute" is not just world-beating brag: it is a description of the boobs of the territory (and therefore a Murkan assessment as well). The costs of world-beating and sitting on the safety-valve are high: setting ourselves up like that, needing to show that whopping the sun is what we can do even when the occasion doesn't call for it. *Murk* is a flattering term for something that does not show what's really going on, but implies that we might rather not find out.

All three artists are political conservatives. This description is perhaps misleading. Not conservative in the manner of conservative Republicans but more in the manner of Edmund Burke. But what's wrong really is the word *political*. And more wrong if I were to say *reactionary*, perhaps a word more descriptive of what these men want, for they do not want to hang on to what they have but yearn for what's already been eliminated from our lives. They don't like what the present seems to be tending them toward. So drop *political* but think "the world they would like to see."

Ives is the most anomalous. He rewrites *He Is There!* for

World War II and the result is antifascist. But there is his proposed populist amendment to the United States Constitution, a scheme to canvass the nation on matters of pressing national concern, his letter to Franklin D. Roosevelt on a similar subject, and his essay "The Majority."[2] He is, in a sense, not so much reactionary as a proper theorist, always impossible to categorize according to the politics of day-to-day men or shadings of popular political journalism. Faulkner writes a letter of remonstration to a black friend and former employee who solicits him for a contribution to the National Association for the Advancement of Colored People.[3] Richard Nixon helps the ailing John Ford to the podium to get his Life Achievement Award from the American Film Institute. Nixon raises Ford's rank in the Naval Reserve from rear admiral to admiral, first as a whim of the moment, later in earnest. Ford gives Nixon a warm salute at another tribute dinner late in his life.[4] Some excusers say that Ford was old and foolish. They ought to remember that this foolish fellow had not that long ago finished *Seven Women*. Others say he was carrying military discipline too far; they should remember that Ford's central political orientation was formed in the years before and during World War II. His military service, military rank, and military loyalty were to him matters of profound seriousness. It was not just that Nixon was commander-in-chief, but that because Ford was an admiral he was *his* commander-in-chief. He describes himself as "an American—apolitical."

But why would such artists end this way, regretting what is here, yearning for what is gone? What is their need to appear above or beyond politics while at the same time they yearn for the intact social fabric, the functioning community of the past? There is a key here to both Amerikey and Murka. For Amerikey there is a position deep in the American grain that calls for us to be ready to summon up a Golden Age now past in order to brag of the fundamental root to our present overwhelming strength; Murka would argue that this strength has fallen off, we are now on a downhill slide, this is not that end,

but promised earnest of an even greater depth to come: therefore we should be up and arming! In a way Ford's darkest
glimpse of this low point of Murka is in *Two Rode Together*, in
the suddenness of the lynching of the Captive Indian/White
Boy and the helplessness of those who stand by the music box.
Faulkner's is, I suppose, either the end of *The Mansion* as all of
Flem's present power cannot buy him any escape from that
past well buried but now resurrected in his Nemesis Mink
Snopes released from prison. Or in the despair inherent in our
realization as readers that Joe Christmas—it is axiomatic—*has*
to take off Joanna Burden's head, for that is what he is, what
he has been made, what he is now inexorably aimed at. Such
examples demonstrate how futile it can be to try to place even
an artist *only* in Amerikey or in Murka.

Faulkner, Ford, and Ives all deal with the issues of both
Amerikey and Murka, and one would never want the Amerikey readings of the canons, the tendency in these artists to
construction and the exploration of new paths (I suppose) to
beauty for the further bragging of the nation, to conceal their
dark dealings on the other side. Faulkner's dark writing came
early in his career, and Ford's films seem darker late in his career, but as I write this another anomaly occurs to me: I think
that the dark side is early and late—Mink Snopes's search for
Flem and his death come late, in *The Mansion*, and the dark
world an instant away from John Carradine's pointed pistol in
Stagecoach and the cries of Joe Boleo on the ramparts of the
stockade in *Drums Along the Mohawk* are both early. Ike Snopes
and Jody Varner in *The Hamlet* are not instances of light-
hearted comedy, nor is the hegira of *The Reivers*. And there is
always darkness in Ford, sometimes just over the horizon,
sometimes in the immediate past, sometimes right at hand.
Ives's dark pieces (*Immortality*, *At Sea*, Nos. 5 and 4 of 114
Songs; the early movements of the *Third Symphony*, *The Unanswered Question*) come early and late, and speak of darkness
that has been and will be again. The use of Indians as subject

matter by all three artists suggests another dark Murkan mood shared.[5] And all this may suggest that their darkness is the most American thing about all three.

Pessimism is not necessarily representative of Murka: dark pieces tend to bright conclusions, to the positive, just because they assert by being art that we can reach through any moment of despair beyond suffering to the possibility of light, possibility of light suggested by the testament of the existence of the song/film/story itself. And we all swing from Murka to Amerikey, caught in our actions suspended somewhere between helpless brag and guilty despair.

Perhaps perversity is more what I want to get at. These very successful artists (they achieved what they set out to do) made some works for themselves which pleased neither critics *nor* public, had "bad box office," moved at some point in their careers away from their usual familiarizing tactics (domesticating the unfamiliar) in order to venture into the uncommunicable, the unreadable, the unwatchable, the unplayable. They still felt these pieces were important to what they were doing, so there is perhaps something to be learned in this working against the grain.

For Ives it is the unplayable keyboard pieces and the unsingable songs. I take the word of my musician friends that some of Ives's music even yet lies beyond the pale of performability and may never (barring some epidemic of virtuosity or miracle of textual emendation) be played, sung, or heard. To write the impossible is, I think, un-American for a democrat—even for an elitist aristocrat it might run against the grain. In the first place to say it is truly unplayable/unsingable/impossible, one must first move to an advanced state of performance skills (the *Concord Sonata* and the *Third Symphony* were once held to be impossible). One reading of what Ives was doing in these pieces is to suggest that only ingenious performance tricks or tactics could make much of Ives (including *Concord*) performable in the first place, that only the clarity of fingering and score manipulation were capable of bringing light to the gloom of the impossible combination and shifty, conflicting, inconsistent tempi and rhythms. I think experience of Ives performances in recent years belies this reading. His music has been performed more and (generally) better since his death than before.

Another way to approach the meaning of the unplayable is to take the reading of Ives which regards his whole canon as the experiment, with *Slow March* at one end of the spectrum, the unplayable songs and pieces at the other: how simple can I get and retain meaning, how difficult and remain possible. This reading would hold that it takes all kinds of difficulties of music to make the whole an experiment: let's see if *all* this can be done by anybody. This reading puts a modern definition on the idea of score if one has been thinking of score only as a code for the music, sitting there in the notes on the page. This new sense of score is that of a challenge, a puzzle without any "correct" solution, a gauntlet thrown down to the performer to make of it what might be made, to get at what might lie beyond what a performer thought himself capable of. To demonstrate that he *cannot* get beyond it accomplishes the score's function and it then becomes the music it wanted to be, evokes what it wanted to evoke: unplayed music now becomes something theoretical like Keats's "unheard" melodies. Experiment at the edge of possible performance shows that possible performance *has* edges, limits, dimensions.

On the other hand (as we Americans are wont to say) the unplayable is the counterpart confronting George Ives's pragmatic musicianship, which took what could be known by the Danbury Band and stretched it, made music for what the Danbury Band might become: what the young Charles Ives was driving at in *America Variations*. Once we had our ears on we could hear all of it, and eventually even the most popular extent of the populace's ears measured up. We know the music of *America Variations* and can whistle its tunes. It is one of the most popular pieces of Ives's music that finds its way into the

background of local programming on public-broadcasting stations. It may have started at Murka, but it now means America, almost Amerikey.

Part of Faulkner's impossible experiment is of a different
kind which some would not call an experiment at all (indeed
the two novels in question won several prizes and have been
thoroughly dealt with in Faulkner criticism). For something
like Ives's "unplayable" music, the testing of the edge of fiction by experiment, the short stories offer the most radical example. "Carcassonne" might stand as Faulkner's closest approach to the narrative next step James Joyce took, if it were
not foolish to compare a short piece like this to *Finnegans
Wake*. "Carcassonne" has an experience of the edges of language, but more significant, of the edges of narrative. *Finnegans Wake* always narrates even when the untrained reader
might conclude it was narrating in gibberish; "Carcassonne"
thought to use style to replace narrative. In doing so Faulkner
was, first and last, a man who wanted to read aloud, not just
for style but to hear members of his audience jump ahead with
his story as he gave them the narrative clues by which they
might advance. He wanted in what he read aloud (that favorite passage from *The Reivers* that he trotted out for years
before he published it) to have the instant gratification of re-
ply from those faces out there in the dark. In what he wrote
and never read out loud he wanted something like this from
those unseen and unknown faces out there in a different kind
of dark. To deny himself narration and retain only allusive-
ness was a denial of that gratification, even as he denied
himself fictional believability in the experiment of "Artist at
Home." His experiment would, in a career so dedicated to
reader response and reader pleasing, have to take in the possibility of reader rejection and frustration, but as deliberate experiment this would most clearly have been against his grain
and ours.

The only option to the preferring of our interest as readers/hearers for both Ives and Faulkner—no matter how extreme their ventures in these experiments—was for them to keep their peace, to maintain silence. This may have been what Ives was up to between 1926 and 1954, whether or not he consciously arrived at noncreation, the silence of no works.

For Ford the impossible is not, as some have said, *Tobacco Road*—that is just laying Fordian touches on top of what a popular tradition of theatre audiences has already overburdened with touches of its own. Rather it is that central enigma *The Fugitive*. "His favorite picture is *Young Mr. Lincoln:* 'I've got a copy of that at home, on 16mm. I run that quite often. . . .' He thought, 'Now, let me see. . . . What other pictures have I got copies of? Not many. . . . *The Lost Patrol*—I still enjoy that one; and I think I may have a copy of *Yellow Ribbon.*' He is fond of *How Green Was My Valley* and *The Fugitive.* ('I just enjoy myself looking at it.')"[6]

Dudley Nichols gives an account of the genesis of this film:

This project we had talked about for years, but no studio would back it. Now Ford was independent, with Merian Cooper [at the formation of Argosy Pictures], and he wanted to do it. I said I was sure it would not make any profit, but I was eager to script it. We soon realized it was impossible to script the Graham Greene novel . . . [*The Power and the Glory* or *The Labyrinthine Way*, 1940], on account of censorship. His novel was of a guilty priest, and we could have thought, and after I had worked at its impossible problems for a while, I suggested writing an allegory of the Passion Play, in modern terms, laid in Mexico, using as much of Greene's story as we dared. Ford liked the idea. I did a long draft but was dissatisfied—on the point of throwing it over. Yet Ford showed enthusiasm, and he came to my office at RKO for about a week or ten days, and from what I had written, and from the novel, and from our own ideas, we redictated the script.[7]

The film was just the failure Nichols predicted, and critics (including Lindsay Anderson, from whose article this quotation is taken) have tended to agree with his judgment. But if the challenge (or aim) of the work was impossibility, if Ford years later could think of himself watching it with (perhaps self-indulgent) pleasure, then *The Fugitive* cannot be dismissed as a dog. I think it isn't. It is slow, massive in its movements and in its underlined religious formalism. Dolores Del Rio seems an oddly cold choice for a Ford heroine, and the characters in general are distanced by their sense of their roles in some movie we cannot see—the allegory or whatever it is that Ford expects this film to embody. It's not a Western, in spite of the familiarity of the Mexican setting: that's avoided in the cobblestone courtyard, used to such good effect on the soundtrack, making something more like a genre unit from a Nazi picture than a genre unit taking its origin from Western. The people of the picture never form themselves into a community, either, but come on and off screen with that apparent predetermination characteristic of the chorus in a very deliberate production of Verdi's *Don Carlo* or *I Vespri Siciliani*.[8] And with the same air of religious hypnosis. And the narrative comes no closer to Greene's spoiled priest—spoilt by booze and sex—than Fritz Lang's *Fury* approaches a philippic about the lynchings of blacks in the South simply by showing some happy blacks in the background through a window in another scene.

But it *is* unmistakably Ford and Fordian throughout, and if it matters to him whether we like what we see in this movie or not, we must find some place for it in the canon and in his efforts and aims. One explanation for it has been to make a critical appeal to Ford's Irish Catholic upbringing, has declared this to be a simple-minded return to simple peasant faith, religious in ways the nonreligious will never be able to understand. That's pretty good vicarious autobiography, but not very good criticism, for it is uncharacteristic of the way Ford's Roman Catholicism emerges in scores of his other films. He is direct when his movies deal with the miraculous and

with God's frustrating of shortsighted human plans, but elsewhere he scrupulously avoids selling us a load of clams.[9]

I think our trouble is not getting right what kind of clams
he is selling. *The Fugitive* is clearly a venture in the purely formal or he never would allow that chorus to move the way it
does or frame it on the screen as he does when it makes one of
those overcued appearances, nor would he permit himself the
blunt appeal to the mute and heavy-handed symbolism of the
silents we see as Fonda's priest first enters the Church. Even
the Christmas pageant of *Donovan's Reef* is closer to doctrinal
Roman Catholic orthodoxy. To assert that *The Fugitive* is un-
digested Catholicism is to confuse ritual and doctrine. It's not
to get at Greene's own message of the guilt of the holy and
holiness of the guilty which the novel so eloquently narrates—
Ford has never found his long suit in narrating the messages of
others. The sense of spoilt priest is inherent in what we see on
the screen in the cleansed version of events the movie uses,
even if Ford had to omit spoilt priest from what we see because
of the Legion of Decency—and I suppose because of his own
feelings about the Church. But this will not account for what
Ford *is* doing. Nor is it that Fonda is miscast as the fugitive
priest: he was in a way miscast in *Young Mr. Lincoln* and still
found his way, perhaps brilliantly. He finds his way in this, even
though the character's distance frustrates many of the devices
we might look for in a more familiar Fonda/Ford collaboration.

I think the experiment here is a combination of the impos-
sibles sought by Ives and Faulkner: the impossibility of "performance"—something that lay beyond Nichols's and Ford's and
Fonda's tricks, thus achieved capability—and the impossibility of Ford's usual language of gesture and human completeness (as in Faulkner's denial of his recourse to narrative), the
fullness of secondary characters, the empathy we grant to Ford
heroes, and the impossibility of ungrounded, unprepared-for
allegory in narrative. In other words, some part of the formal
as it becomes divorced from its supporting substance, that sub-

stance which customarily supports the formal in Ford's experiments and in a way sanctions form: the weight in substance lends the unfamiliar formal matter he gives us.

All three dwell on old tunes: Ives turns us to our folk, our religious, our patriotic past to hear again, as in the now vanished, distant, and lonesome whistles of the freight train, the tunes of a past, Ives's and our own, reset. Faulkner, in several revival meetings in *The Sound and the Fury*, now bereft of their power to reinstill awe or fear; in the several agonizing realizations that novel brings us to that the dwindling is not yet over and done with, will run on yet for a good long time, will have to be endured. Ford, in the *Red River Valley* and *Shall We Gather at the River?* prayers and hymns at setting out, hope in hymns at buryings, the memory of being together in a community which isn't any more.

These old tunes are a ground bass, not altogether mournful, in the midst of our Murka, of an ideal America which is cultural constant to the variable of aesthetic, formal, narrative, sequential experiment. *Bringing in the Sheaves* and *Down in the Cornfield* (*Massa's in de Cold, Cold Ground*), *Shall We Gather at the River?*, the flags at the corners of the raw lumber of Tombstone's new church, the Stevenson poem "Home Is the Sailor" at the alien graveside far in the Philippines, Gavin Stevens's long look at his town—all speak to something suspended between the American grain and against the grain, between Amerikey and Murka, between frontier boast and Age of Anxiety despair.[10]

But against what grain: against the grain of either of the other two artists' work. I have been stressing similarities and parallels so much that I might thus far stand accused of trying to prove something I said was absurd early on: to try to prove all three are the same artist. They are not. Each took a different road and those three roads made a great deal of difference. The different road, though, was not just the different art or the difference between the state of letters, music, and film each found at his apprenticeship or at his apogee, but a perhaps more significant difference in road.

It was once the fashion to regard arts as lowbrow, middlebrow, and highbrow, signifying I suppose the level at which the hairline met the forehead, the lowest for the equivalent of a Neanderthal, the highest for a domed egghead.[11] Low, middle, and high art are different from -brows and somewhat better targeted in definition, for they turn ultimately not on intent but on audience. Low art (and it is a prejudicial term) is popular culture or something a little more difficult, popular art. Middle art is just that, middle—in between low and high. High art competes with the Greeks or with the Renaissance or with whatever art the art- and music- and literary-historians tell us is up there with the biggies.

I have been suggesting in this book that we have been too restrictive and exlusionist in our criticism as we chose which art to talk about, regarding high art as *it* and all others as somehow beyond the pale or—an even more convenient ruse—as something *else*, something different, not to be judged to be in the same ball game.

If we took the high-, low-, and middle- categories uncritically I should think that movies tend to be low, literature and music tend to be high. Literature can of course be middle or perhaps low, depending on how it sells. Music chooses its own poison and tends to predetermine its audience by the "kind" it chooses to be: punk, hard rock, concert, popular, folk, art, national, or whatever.

Opera has a popularity which makes Verdi different—at least in his initial sense of his audience—from Strauss in his initial sense of his. But there is communication from one to another of these apparently hard and fast boundaries, particularly in America. There's a structural difference that goes along with this. Hymns are not symphonies. *Saturday Evening Post* stories are not *Partisan Review* stories. *The New Yorker* falls between stools but it doesn't think it does; and documentaries are not fiction films because they have not only different origins but different formal structures. For movies the European taste is by some thought to designate high art in film. (Is it like Bergman? Ford when asked about Bergman always pretended to confuse Ingmar with Ingrid and answer as if Ingrid had been meant, just to spite the questioner. Of course the irony is that Ingmar Bergman, like the rest, thinks Ford one of the greatest directors.) Ford's films were subject for years to the Selznick fallacy, something like the European bias—assuming that *The Informer* and *The Grapes of Wrath*, since they were evaluable by European standards, were the only films by Ford worthy of serious attention.

"Worthy of serious attention" is the rub. One would think that the high-art folks would want to pay some serious attention to the art the middle of their nation was paying some mind to (and paying some hard-earned bucks for)—that perhaps this might be worthy of wider attention than that of a few inveterate gallery- or concertgoers. The serious attention paid by the artist to his work is, of course, never what they are talking about. Norman Mailer has long straddled low and high, written high in a low manner (*Of a Fire on the Moon*) and low in the high style (*The Executioner's Song*). In the initial instance of this attempt, at the time of his contract with *Esquire*, he was attempting to point out the kinship fiction-writers ought to feel with their origins in Dickens, that fiction used to be "what maids read," that the challenge match of meeting a deadline was more a part of fiction's tradition than was the Nobel Prize for Literature. Film criticism has been of some use in breaking down this prejudice. There was always a band of certain Ford enthusiasts, even in the face of distractions such as *Informer* snobbery, European bias, and reviewers who found that masterworks such as *Two Rode Together* and *Cheyenne Autumn* put them off, represented (they felt) an old man past his prime.

No matter what the failures of the high-middle-low art system, if we use it as a grid to suggest something about these three artists it brings us to a nice—perhaps even a conclusive—ambivalent comparison. All three artists wrote all three: Faulkner wrote for the *Saturday Evening Post* and *Argosy* and newspapers, did book-club best sellers, and published in limited editions by private publishers stories he did not place elsewhere. He never had any doubt he was popular, nor did the public or for that matter the National Book Award committee, and he never worried for more than a few moments whether he was serious (the introductory comments to the old edition of *Sanctuary* being one of those rare occasions[12]), and neither did the Nobel Prize and the Pulitzer Prize committees. Ives had the Pulitzer as well, but giving it to him rather risked the committee's credibility as representatives of some level of visibility. His songs touch the lowbrow but do not belong there in use or popularity or in the medium of their dispersal. Middle he perhaps never willingly was. But this survey should not ignore the popular song, hymn, patriotic tune that he makes into melodic and rhythmic and motival content, for these make it possible for him to penetrate the audiences for low and middle. I have heard Ives on the kind of Muzak for tired businessmen that is piped to every seat on an airplane: if that's not near-low I don't know what is. Ford's Academy Awards and his box-office records show he had the low and middle, and *The Informer* and *The Grapes of Wrath* are treated with respect by solemn film historians even early on; Paul Rotha in 1935 makes much of *The Iron Horse*.[13]

But if we were to use the same documentary evidence to show the contrast between the three it would be clear that Ives took the high road—could not be recognized until *New Music* published his pieces and they got played in Town Hall; Ford took the low road and his pictures played the Last Picture Show of every hick town in the country; Faulkner fell somewhere in between: too popular to be taken up by the academics until somewhere in the late Forties and Fifties (in short-story collections and American survey courses) and not turning up in cultural rundowns of Literature Between the Wars (as we were to come to call it so awkwardly) until later in the

same decade, but eventually making it into a high-art pan-
theon with Washington Irving and Herman Melville and (almost as overdue as Faulkner) Mark Twain.

The ambivalence speaks to the theme I put in my Prologue,
American ambivalence. Art should be for the people, but on
the other hand (Emerson says) we should have artists of our
own to stack up against the universe. If we do, won't they become *artists* and thus undemocratic? But if they go on making popular stuff won't they fail to measure up to our Older
Sibling?

Fortunately this kind of alternate questioning between arms
of an ambivalence bothers this straw man of American taste
more than it would P. T. Barnum *or* Thomas Eakins. Faulkner, Ford, and Ives all found Nature (in Eakins's term) and
used that "canoe" to travel to, to paint the light; all three—to
Barnum's satisfaction, I trust—whopped the sun. All three
did their (each his own) thing and found ways within this and
within the guidelines for fiction, film, and music to do something wholly, astonishingly new. And all three have no successful imitative following. *The Searchers* has a huge following
of *hommages*—filmed replicas of its incidents or characters or
structures.[13] The Faulknerian style has been taken up (and
dropped) by first-novelists ever since, and high-music composers have thought they were following Ives when they repli-
cated once again American music's habit of pastiche—but
they were not. They could not. They hadn't even figured out
how astonishing what he did was.

The wonder of the world. But Ford says, "Well, I like making them, of course. . . . But it's no use asking me to talk
about art." Faulkner says, "The carpenter don't build a house
just to drive nails. He drives nails to build a house." Ives says,
"To see the sunrise a man has but to get up early, and he can
always have Bach in his pocket."

Look at these three faces—mask, icon, disguise.
William Faulkner had two portraits: a later one, frank and

nearly jolly, certain and approachable, the tolerant question-answerer, smiling from behind the podium at U. Va., the smoke-blowing elder statesman being lionized at his nation's Military Academy, all duded up in fancy dress. The other is early, the look of the reporter of *Pylon*, tweed coat, veiled and vaguely hostile expression, shadowed and impatient for the sitting to end. This (in an unshadowed version) is the image cultivated by him for his first *Time* cover, galluses at the ready to be snapped, khaki work shirt implying some service now past, the eyes giving nothing away, offering no clue to what *he* thinks of having his picture taken other than that right now he is barely tolerating it.

Both portraits correspond to what people who knew Faulkner inevitably say if you ask them: either they call him Bill (as Bennett Cerf did) and speak of affability (in contrast to the reputation for distance and unreachable greatness), or they tell of seeing him across a room drinking at a cocktail party, drinking at some foreign diplomatic post, isolating himself behind that veil of the eyes, laconic to strangers. The good film evidence is a program done for *Omnibus* shortly after the Nobel Prize announcement, which follows Faulkner as he re-enacts the day after he got the news of the prize. Faulkner calls on his friends, stops by the Courthouse Square, delivers at his daughter's high-school graduation exercises a version of the Nobel Prize speech. Never do we see more in the eyes which give nothing away, the mask that will not be raised.

The image of Ives seems silent, a rending stare in the photographs taken late in life, an image of relentlessness determined to emerge from the photo and affect us who are looking at it. Spookily powerful, he stares out of aloneness even when the photo also includes Harmony his wife and it is the spiritual aloneness this stare portends that perhaps speaks to the late functions of himself—the surviving artist who has abdicated the act of making art—as icon for his own work. Marcel Duchamp stops making art to become himself his own chief—his only current—work. Plays chess. And is still around. Ives was certainly in fear and probably in peril of his life when these pictures were taken, but this does not explain, or even adequately address, what we see. The stare is that of a man become something other than a maker or a doer, become a representative of his own distance from this world, a stare isolating himself from society and from the encroaching relationship of human swamps all those around him would make of his time and space. Stanley Cavell writes that in seeing movies we contemplate a world without ourselves, and it is perhaps this that Ives sees in these stares, apart from other artists, then from the insurance business of his other career, finally apart from making any new music. This is not Duchamp, but it is not Ford or Faulkner, either. Ives is not sliding into failure or stasis but awaiting the call. The stare and the icon demonstrate the aloneness his music itself provides us, without the necessity, as he here demonstrates, for it to need a composer any more.

Ford is in disguise, first behind green spectacles like the aging Wordsworth, seeming farther away than he really is, seeming that way by device: disguised for what the disguise can accomplish for him. Human swamps are what Hollywood is, they say. Then he adds an eyepatch to the green spectacles. Disguise upon disguise. Not only did his waking days always feature them and their problems, but on them rested the responsibility to get what he saw in his head onto the screen: only through these people (see *memo from: David O. Selznick*) would he be able to make art. The disguise was the calculating distance of the military commander: if you're going to go out there and die I don't want to get to know you very well, and if I've got to send you you can't get to know me very well. Of the helpful organizer who just wanted to keep the company together and do what was best for all (the anonymous nonartist). Of the blind man who might not (but always did) see what you were trying to get away with. And there was just a little plea for sympathy for the man in so obviously visual an art, for the man who cannot see, who makes us see: magic. He is shaman and the eye patch is his badge. And the glasses it covers. And the hats with the deep brims.

According to the several accounts of his work given us by individual stars of the first magnitude—O'Hara and Fonda and Stewart and Marvin and Wayne—the disguise, even though they knew that that's what it was, worked.

It was also, of course, as all disguises and masks are, a way of saying it is not me but my work you must look at. And this is the most important contrast to the late-life icon of Charles Ives, which stared at us to gather our lesser stares back again, at him.

Faulkner knew it was all in the work, and didn't think that once he was behind the mask he had to tell us again. Ives thought it was all in the work, but he had to turn himself into an icon, to get us to see it. Ford just kept on his working-stiff disguise, the eye patch as work clothes, because he kept on working at it until he died.

That they all had to cultivate these poses or responses, had to invent what they were to look like, had to appear once they were artists to be something else, one way or another, is American. It's only one reason that to be an original in America is so difficult and so rare.

APPENDICES

THE PRINCIPAL WORKS

I have listed here the principal works of each artist, omitting titles not relevant to this book.

WILLIAM FAULKNER

Absalom, Absalom! New York: Random House, 1936.

As I Lay Dying. New York: Cape and Smith, 1936; Random House.

Collected Stories. New York: Random House, 1950.

A Fable. New York: Random House, 1954.

The Hamlet. New York: Random House, 1940.

Intruder in the Dust. New York: Random House, 1948.

Knight's Gambit. New York: Random House, 1949.

Light in August. New York: Smith and Haas, 1932; Random House.

The Mansion. New York: Random House, 1959.

The Marble Faun. Boston: Four Seas Co., 1924; Random House, to-gether with *A Green Bough.*

Mosquitoes. New York: Boni & Liveright, 1926; Random House.

The Portable Faulkner. Edited by Malcolm Cowley. New York: Viking, 1946.

Pylon. New York: Smith and Haas, 1935; Random House.

The Reivers. New York: Random House, 1962.

Requiem for a Nun. New York: Random House, 1951.

Sanctuary. New York: Cape and Smith, 1929; Random House.

Sartoris. New York: Harcourt, Brace, 1929; Random House.

The Sound and the Fury. New York: Cape and Smith, 1929; Random House.

These Thirteen. New York: Cape and Smith, 1939.

The Town. New York: Random House, 1957.

The Unvanquished. New York: Random House, 1938.

The Wild Palms. New York: Random House, 1939.

INTERVIEWS WITH FAULKNER

Faulkner at Nagano. Edited by Robert A. Jelliffe. Tokyo: Kenkyusha Ltd., 1956. Most of this was later included in *Lion in the Garden.*

Faulkner at West Point. Edited by Joseph L. Fant and Robert Ashley. New York: Random House, 1964.

Faulkner in the University. Edited by Frederick L. Gwynn and Joseph L. Blotner. Charlottesville: The University of Virginia Press, 1959; Random House.

Lion in the Garden: Interviews with William Faulkner 1926–1962. Edited by James B. Meriwether and Michael Millgate. New York: Random House, 1968.

JOHN FORD

The Tornado, 1917 (released 3 March) Universal–101 Bison). Director-writer: Jack Ford. With Jack Ford, Jean Hathaway, John Duffy, Pete Gerald, Elsie Thompson. 2 reels.

Straight Shooting, 1917 (released 27 August) (Butterfly-Universal). Director: Jack Ford. Writer: George Hively. Photographer: George Scott. With Harry Carey, Molly Malone, Duke Lee, Vester Pegg, Hoot Gibson. 5 reels. Ford's first feature.

Napoleon's Barber, 1928 (released 24 November). (Fox-Movietone). Director: John Ford. Scenarist: Arthur Caesar, from his own play. Photographer: George Schneiderman. With Otto Matiesen, Frank Reicher, Natalie Golitzin, Helen Ware, Philippe De Lacy. 32 minutes. Ford's first talkie.

Black Watch, 1929 (released 22 May) (Fox). Directors: John Ford ("staged by" Lumsden Hare). Scenarists: James Kevin McGuinness, John Stone, from Talbot Mundy's novel, *King of the Khyber Rifles.* Photographer: John H. August. Editor: Alex Troffey. With Victor McLaglen, Myrna Loy, Roy D'Arcy, David Rollins, Francis Ford. 93 minutes.

The Lost Patrol, 1934 (released 16 February) (RKO Radio). Director: John Ford. Executive producer: Merian C. Cooper. Scenarists: Dudley Nichols, Garrett Fort, from Philip MacDonald's story, "Patrol." Photographer: Harold Wenstrom. Art directors: Van Nest Polglase, Sidney Ullman. Music: Max Steiner. Editor: Paul Weatherwax. Filmed in the Yuma desert. With Victor McLaglen,

Boris Karloff, Wallace Ford, Reginald Denny, Alan Hale. 74 minutes.

Judge Priest, 1934 (released 5 October) (Fox). Director: John Ford. Producer: Sol Wurtzel. Scenarists: Dudley Nichols, Lamar Trotti, from Irvin S. Cobb's stories. Photographer: George Schneiderman. Music: Samuel Kaylin. With Will Rogers, Henry B. Walthall, Tom Brown, Anita Louise, Rochelle Hudson, Charley Grapewin, Francis Ford. 80 minutes.

The Informer, 1935 (released 1 May) (RKO Radio). Director: John Ford. Scenarist: Dudley Nichols, from Liam O'Flaherty's novel. Photographer: Joseph H. August. Art directors: Van Nest Polglase, Charles Kirk. Music: Max Steiner. Editor: George Hively. With Victor McLaglen, Heather Angel, Preston Foster, Wallace Ford, Una O'Connor, Donald Meek, Francis Ford. 91 minutes.

Steamboat Round the Bend, 1935 (released 6 September) (20th Century–Fox). Director: John Ford. Producer: Sol M. Wurtzel. Scenarists: Dudley Nichols, Lamar Trotti, from Ben Lucian Burman's story. Photographer: George Schneiderman. Art director: William Darling. Editor: Alfred De Gaetano. With Will Rogers, Anne Shirley, Eugene Pallette, John McGuire, Berton Churchill, Stepin' Fetchit, Francis Ford, Irvin S. Cobb, Jack Pennick. 80 minutes.

The Prisoner of Shark Island, 1936 (released 12 February) (20th Century–Fox). Director: John Ford. Producer: Darryl F. Zanuck. Associate producer–scenarist: Nunnally Johnson, from the life of Doctor Samuel A. Mudd. Photography: Bert Glennon. Art director: William Darling. Editor: Jack Murray. With Warner Baxter, Gloria Stuart, Claude Gillingwater, Harry Carey, John Carradine, Francis Ford, Frank McGlynn, Sr., Francis McDonald, Jack Pennick. 95 minutes.

Wee Willie Winkie, 1937 (released 30 July) (20th Century–Fox). Director: John Ford. Producer: Darryl F. Zanuck. Scenarists: Ernest Pascal, Julian Josephson, from Rudyard Kipling's story. Photography: Arthur Miller. Music: Louis Silvers. Editor: Walter Thompson. With Shirley Temple, Victor McLaglen, C. Aubrey Smith, June Lang, Cesar Romero. 99 minutes.

The Hurricane, 1937 (released 24 December) (Goldwyn–United Artists). Director: John Ford. Producer: Samuel Goldwyn. Scenarist: Dudley Nichols from novel by Charles Nordhoff and James Norman Hall, adapted by Oliver H. P. Garrett. Hurricane sequence: James Basevi. Photography: Bert Glennon, Archie Stout (second-unit). Art directors: Richard Day, Alex Golitzen. Music: Alfred Newman. Editor: Lloyd Nosler. Exterior locations at Samoa. With Dorothy Lamour, Jon Hall, Mary Astor, C. Aubrey Smith, Thomas Mitchell, Raymond Massey, John Carradine, Jerome Cowan, Al Kikume, Movita Castenada. 102 minutes.

Stagecoach, 1939 (released 2 March) (Wanger–United Artists). Director-producer: John Ford. Executive producer: Walter Wanger. Scenarist: Dudley Nichols, from Ernest Haycox's story, "Stage to Lordsburg." Photographer: Bert Glennon. Art director: Alexander Toluboff. Music: from folk tunes of early 1880's. Editors: Dorothy Spencer, Walter Reynolds. Filmed in Monument Valley and other locations in Arizona, Utah, California. With John Wayne, Claire Trevor, John Carradine, Thomas Mitchell, Andy Devine, Donald Meek, Louise Platt, Tim Holt, George Bancroft, Francis Ford, Jack Pennick. 97 minutes.

Young Mr. Lincoln, 1939 (released 9 June) (Cosmopolitan–20th Century–Fox). Director: John Ford. Executive producer: Darryl F. Zanuck. Producer: Kenneth Macgowan. Scenarist: Lamar Trotti, based on life of Abraham Lincoln. Photography: Bert Glennon. Art directors: Richard Day, Mark Lee Kirk. Music: Alfred Newman. Editor: Walter Thompson. With Henry Fonda, Alice Brady, Marjorie Weaver, Arleen Whelan, Eddie Collins, Pauline Moor, Ward Bond, Donald Meek, Eddie Quillan, Francis Ford, Russell Simpson. 101 minutes.

Drums Along the Mohawk, 1939 (released 3 November) (20th Century–Fox). Director: John Ford. Executive producer: Darryl F. Zanuck. Producer: Raymond Griffith. Scenarists: Lamar Trotti, Sonya Levien, from Walter D. Edmonds's novel. Photography (in Technicolor): Bert Glennon, Ray Rennahan. Art directors: Richard Day, Mark Lee Kirk. Music: Alfred Newman. Editor: Robert Simpson. With Claudette Colbert, Henry Fonda, Edna May Oliver, Eddie Collins, John Carradine, Jessie Ralph, Arthur Shields, Ward Bond, Russell Simpson, Francis Ford, Chief Big Tree, Jack Pennick, Mae Marsh. 103 minutes.

The Grapes of Wrath, 1940 (released 15 March) (20th Century–Fox). Director: John Ford. Producer: Darryl F. Zanuck. Associate producer–scenarist: Nunnally Johnson, from John Steinbeck's novel. Photography: Gregg Tolland. Art directors: Richard Day, Mark Lee Kirk. Music: Alfred Newman (song, *Red River Valley*, played on accordion by Dan Borzage). With Henry Fonda, Jane

Darwell, John Carradine, Charley Grapewin, Dorris Bowdon, Russell Simpson, John Qualen, Eddie Quillan, Ward Bond, Mae Marsh, Francis Ford, Jack Pennick. 129 minutes.

The Long Voyage Home, 1940 (released 8 October) (Wanger–United Artists). Director: John Ford. Producer: Walter Wanger. Scenarist: Dudley Nichols, from Eugene O'Neill's one-act plays, *The Moon of the Caribbees*, *In the Zone*, *Bound East for Cardiff*, *The Long Voyage Home*. Photography: Gregg Toland. Art director: James Basevi. Music: Richard Hageman. Editor: Sherman Todd. With Thomas Mitchell, John Wayne, Ian Hunter, Barry Fitzgerald, Wilfred Lawson, Mildred Natwick, John Qualen, Ward Bond, Arthur Shields, Jack Pennick, Dan Borzage. 105 minutes.

Tobacco Road, 1941 (released 20 February) (20th Century–Fox). Director: John Ford. Producer: Darryl F. Zanuck. Scenarist: Nunnally Johnson, from Jack Kirkland's play and Erskine Caldwell's novel. Photography: Arthur C. Miller. Art directors: Richard Day, James Basevi. Music: David Buttolph. Editor: Barbara McLean. With Charley Grapewin, Marjorie Rambeau, Gene Tierney, William Tracy, Elizabeth Patterson, Slim Summerville, Ward Bond, Jack Pennick, Francis Ford. 84 minutes.

How Green Was My Valley, 1941 (released in December) (20th Century–Fox). Director: John Ford. Producer: Darryl F. Zanuck. Scenarist: Philip Dunne, from Richard Llewellyn's novel. Photography: Arthur Miller. Art directors: Richard Day, Nathan Juran. Music: Alfred Newman. Editor: James B. Clark. With Walter Pidgeon, Maureen O'Hara, Donald Crisp, Anna Lee, Roddy McDowall, John Loder, Sara Allgood, Mae Marsh. 118 minutes.

The Battle of Midway, 1942 (released in September) (U.S. Navy–20th Century–Fox). Director-photographer (in color): LCDR John Ford, USNR. Narration written by John Ford, Dudley Nichols, James Kevin McGuinness. Music: Alfred Newman. Editors: John Ford, Robert Parrish. With the voices of Henry Fonda, Jane Darwell, Donald Crisp. 20 minutes.

December 7th, 1943 (U.S. Navy). Directors: Lt. Gregg Toland, USNR, LCDR John Ford, USNR. Photography: Gregg Toland. Music: Alfred Newman. Editor: Robert Parrish. 20 minutes.

They Were Expendable, 1945 (released 20 December) (Metro-Goldwyn-Mayer). Director-producer: John Ford. Scenarist: Frank W. Wead, from William L. White's book. Photography: Joseph H. August. Art directors: Cedric Gibbons, Malcolm F. Brown. Music: Herbert Stothart. Editors: Frank E. Hull, Douglas Biggs. With

Robert Montgomery, John Wayne, Donna Reed, Ward Bond, Marshall Thompson, Russell Simpson, Jack Pennick. 136 minutes.

My Darling Clementine, 1946 (released in November) (20th Century–Fox). Director: John Ford. Producer: Samuel G. Engel. Scenarists: Samuel G. Engel, Winston Miller, from Sam Hellman's story based on Stuart N. Lake's book, *Wyatt Earp, Frontier Marshal*. Photography: Joseph P. MacDonald. Art directors: James Basevi, Lyle R. Wheeler. Music: Cyril J. Mockridge. Editor: Dorothy Spencer. Exteriors filmed in Monument Valley. With Henry Fonda, Linda Darnell, Victor Mature, Walter Brennan, Tim Holt, Ward Bond, Cathy Downs, Alan Mowbray, Jane Darwell, Russell Simpson, Francis Ford, J. Farrell McDonald, Jack Pennick, Mae Marsh. 97 minutes.

The Fugitive, 1947 (released 3 November) (Argosy Pictures–RKO Radio). Director: John Ford. Producers: John Ford, Merian C. Cooper. Scenarist: Dudley Nichols, from Graham Greene's novel *The Labyrinthine Ways*. Photography: Gabriel Figueroa. Art director: Alfred Ybarra. Music: Richard Hageman. Editor: Jack Murray. Executive assistant: Jack Pennick. Filmed in 47 days on locations in Mexico and at Churubusco Studios, Mexico City. With Henry Fonda, Dolores Del Rio, Pedro Armendariz, Ward Bond, J. Carroll Nasih. 104 minutes.

Fort Apache, 1948 (released 9 March) (Argosy Pictures–RKO Radio). Director: John Ford. Producers: John Ford, Merian C. Cooper. Scenarist: Frank S. Nugent, from James Warner Bellah's story "Massacre." Photography: Archie Stout. Art director: James Basevi. Music: Richard Hageman. Assistant directors: Lowell Farrell, Jack Pennick. Filmed in 45 days on locations in Utah and in Monument Valley. With John Wayne, Henry Fonda, Shirley Temple, John Agar, Ward Bond, George O'Brien, Victor McLaglen, Pedro Armendariz, Anna Lee, Irene Rich, Mae Marsh, Francis Ford, Movita Castenada. 127 minutes.

Three Godfathers, 1948 (released 1 December) (Argosy Pictures–Metro-Goldwyn-Mayer). Director: John Ford. Producers: John Ford, Merian C. Cooper. Scenarists: Laurence Stallings, Frank S. Nugent, from story by Peter B. Kyne (a remake of Ford's *Marked Men*, a silent of 1919, and dedicated to its star, Harry Carey). Photography (in color): Winton C. Hoch, Charles P. Boyle (second-unit). Art director: James Basevi. Music: Richard Hageman. Editor: Jack Murray. Filmed in 32 days on locations in the Mojave Desert. With John Wayne, Pedro Armendariz, (introduc-

ing) Harry Carey, Jr., Ward Bond, Mildred Natwick, Jane Darwell, Mae Marsh, Guy Kibbee, Ben Johnson, Jack Pennick, Francis Ford. 106 minutes.

She Wore a Yellow Ribbon, 1949 (released 22 October) (Argosy Pictures–RKO Radio). Director: John Ford. Producers: Ford, Merian C. Cooper. Scenarists: Frank S. Nugent, Laurence Stallings,
from James Warner Bellah's story "War Party." Photography (in
color): Winton C. Hoch, Charles P. Boyle (second-unit). Art director: James Basevi. Music: Richard Hageman. Editor: Jack Murray. Filmed in 31 days on locations in Monument Valley. With
John Wayne, Joanne Dru, John Agar, Ben Johnson, Harry Carey,
Jr., Victor McLaglen, Mildred Natwick, George O'Brien, Arthur
Shields, Francis Ford, Chief Big Tree, Jack Pennick. 103 minutes.

Wagon Master, 1950 (released 19 April) (Argosy Pictures–RKO Ra-
dio). Director: John Ford. Producers: John Ford, Merian C.
Cooper. Writers: Frank S. Nugent, Patrick Ford. Photography:
Bert Glennon, Archie Stout (second-unit). Art director: James
Basevi. Music: Richard Hageman (songs sung by the Sons of the
Pioneers). Editor: Jack Murray. Filmed in Monument Valley and
Professor Valley, Utah. With Ben Johnson, Harry Carey, Jr.,
Joanne Dru, Ward Bond, Charles Kemper, Alan Mowbray, Jane
Darwell, Russell Simpson, Francis Ford. 86 minutes.

Rio Grande, 1950 (released 15 November) (Argosy Pictures–
Republic). Director: John Ford. Producers: John Ford, Merian C.
Cooper. Scenarist: James Kevin McGuinness, from James Warner
Bellah's story "Mission with No Record." Photography: Bert
Glennon, Archie Stout (second-unit). Art director: Frank Hotal-
ing. Music: Victor Young (songs sung by the Sons of the Pioneers).
Editor: Jack Murray. With John Wayne, Maureen O'Hara, Ben
Johnson, Claude Jarman, Jr., Harry Carey, Jr., Chill Wills,
J. Carroll Naish, Victor McLaglen, Grant Withers, Jack Pennick,
Pat Wayne. 105 minutes.

What Price Glory?, 1952 (released in August) (20th Century–Fox).
Director: John Ford. Producer: Sol C. Siegel. Scenarists: Phoebe
and Henry Ephron, from Maxwell Anderson's and Laurence Stallings's play. Photography (in color): Joseph MacDonald. Art directors: Lyle R. Wheeler, George W. Davis. Music: Alfred Newman. Editor: Dorothy Spencer. With James Cagney, Corinne
Calvet, Dan Dailey, William Demarest, Robert Wagner, Marisa
Pavan, James Gleason, Dan Borzage. 111 minutes.

The Quiet Man, 1952 (released 14 September) (Argosy Pictures–Republic). Director: John Ford. Producers: John Ford, Merian C. Cooper. Scenarist: Frank S. Nugent, from Maurice Walsh's story. Photography (in color): Winton C. Hoch, Archie Stout (second-unit). Art director: Frank Hotaling. Music: Victor Young. Editor: Jack Murray. Second-unit directors (uncredited): John Wayne, Patrick Ford. Assistant director: Andrew McLaglen. Exteriors filmed in Ireland. With John Wayne, Maureen O'Hara, Barry Fitzgerald, Ward Bond, Victor McLaglen, Mildred Natwick, Francis Ford, Arthur Shields, Mae Marsh, Patrick Wayne, Antonia Wayne, Melinda Wayne. 129 minutes.

The Sun Shines Bright, 1953 (released 2 May) (Republic). Director: John Ford. Producers: Ford, Merian C. Cooper. Scenarist: Laurence Stallings, from Irvin S. Cobb's stories, "The Sun Shines Bright," "The Mob from Massac," "The Lord Provides." Art director: Frank Hotaling. Music: Victor Young. Editor: Jack Murray. With Charles Winninger, Arleen Whelan, John Russell, Stepin' Fetchit, Russell Simpson, Ludwig Stossel, Francis Ford, Mae Marsh, Jane Darwell, Jack Pennick, Patrick Wayne. 90 minutes. See *Judge Priest*, 1934.

Mogambo, 1953 (released 9 October) (Metro-Goldwyn-Mayer). Director: John Ford. Producer: Sam Zimbalist. Scenarist: John Lee Mahin, from Wilson Collison's play, *Red Dust*. Photography (in color): Robert Surtees, Fredrick A. Young. Art director: Alfred Junge. Editor: Frank Clark. Exteriors filmed in Africa. With Clark Gable, Ava Gardner, Grace Kelly, Donald Sinden, Philip Stainton. 116 minutes.

The Long Gray Line, 1955 (released 9 February) (Rota Productions–Columbia). Director: John Ford. Producer: Robert Arthur. Scenarist: Edward Hope, from Marty Maher's (with Nardi Reeder) autobiography, *Bringing Up the Brats*. Photography (in color and CinemaScope): Charles Lawton, Jr. Art director: Robert Peterson. Music adaptation: George Duning. With Tyrone Power, Maureen O'Hara, Robert Francis, Donald Crisp, Ward Bond, Betsy Palmer, Phil Carey, Harry Carey, Jr., Patrick Wayne, Willis Bouchey, Jack Pennick. 138 minutes.

The Searchers, 1956 (released 26 May) (C. V. Whitney Pictures–Warner Brothers). Director: John Ford. Producers: Merian C. Cooper, C. V. Whitney. Associate producer: Patrick Ford. Photography (in color and Vista-Vision): Winton C. Hoch, Alfred Gilks (second-unit). Art directors: Frank Hotaling, James Basevi.

Music: Max Steiner. Editor: Jack Murray. Filmed in Colorado and Monument Valley. With John Wayne, Jeffrey Hunter, Vera Miles, Ward Bond, Natalie Wood, John Qualen, Olive Carey, Ken Curtis, Harry Carey, Jr., Hank Worden, Pat Wayne, Jack Pennick, Mae Marsh, Dan Borzage. 119 minutes.

The Wings of Eagles, 1957 (released 22 February) (Metro-Goldwyn-Mayer). Director: John Ford. Producer: Charles Schnee. Scenarists: Frank Fenton, William Wister Haines, based on life and writings of CDR Frank W. Wead, USN. Art directors: William A. Horning, Malcolm Brown. Music: Jeff Alexander. With John Wayne, Maureen O'Hara, Dan Dailey, Ward Bond, Ken Curtis, Sig Ruman, Willis Bouchey, Dan Borzage, Jack Pennick, Mae Marsh. 110 minutes.

The Horse Soldiers, 1959 (released in June) (Mirisch Company–United Artists). Director: John Ford. Producers-scenarists: John Lee Mahin, Martin Rackin, from Harold Sinclair's novel. Photography (in color): William H. Clothier. Art director: Frank Hotaling. Music: David Buttolph. Editor: Jack Murray. Filmed in Louisiana and Mississippi. With John Wayne, William Holden, Constance Towers, Althea Gibson, Hoot Gibson, Anna Lee, Russell Simpson, Carleton Young, Basil Ruysdael, Willis Bouchey, Ken Curtis, O. Z. Whitehead, Jack Pennick, Dan Borzage. 119 minutes.

Sergeant Rutledge, 1960 (released in May) (Ford Productions–Warner Brothers). Director: John Ford. Producers: Patrick Ford, Willis Goldbeck. Writers: Willis Goldbeck, James Warner Bellah. Photography (in color): Bert Glennon. Art director: Eddie Imazu. Music: Howard Jackson. Filmed in Monument Valley. With Jeffrey Hunter, Constance Towers, Woody Strode, Billie Burke, Juano Hernandez, Willis Bouchey, Carleton Young, Mae Marsh, Jack Pennick. 111 minutes.

Two Rode Together, 1961 (released in July) (Ford-Shpetner Productions–Columbia). Director: John Ford. Producer: Stan Shpetner. Scenarist: Frank Nugent, from Will Cook's novel, *Comanche Captives*. Photography (in color): Charles Lawton, Jr. Art director: Robert Peterson. Music: George Duning. Editor: Jack Murray. Filmed in southwestern Texas. With James Stewart, Richard Widmark, Shirley Jones, Linda Cristal, Andy Devine, Willis Bouchey, Henry Brandon, Harry Carey, Jr., Ken Curtis, Anna Lee, Ford Rainey, Woody Strode, Jack Pennick, Dan Borzage. 109 minutes.

The Man Who Shot Liberty Valance, 1962 (released in April) (Ford Productions–Paramount). Director: John Ford. Producer: Willis Goldbeck. Scenarists: Goldbeck, James Warner Bellah, from Dorothy M. Johnson's story. Photography: William H. Clothier. Art directors: Hal Pereira, Eddie Imazu. Music: Cyril J. Mockridge; theme from *Young Mr. Lincoln* by Alfred Newman. Editor: Otho Lovering. With James Stewart, John Wayne, Vera Miles, Lee Marvin, Edmond O'Brien, Ken Murray, John Carradine, Willis Bouchey, Carleton Young, Woody Strode, Strother Martin, Jack Pennick. 122 minutes.

Donovan's Reef, 1963 (released in July) (Ford Productions–Paramount). Director-producer: John Ford. Scenarists: Frank Nugent, James Edward Grant, from Edmund Beloin's story, adapted by James Michener. Photography (in color): William Clothier. Art directors: Hal Pereira, Eddie Imazu. Music: Cyril J. Mockridge. Editor: Otho Lovering. Filmed on the island of Kauai in the South Pacific. With John Wayne, Lee Marvin, Elizabeth Allen, Jack Warden, Cesar Romero, Dorothy Lamour, Marcel Dalio, Mae Marsh. 109 minutes.

Cheyenne Autumn, 1964 (released in October) (Ford-Smith Productions–Warner Brothers). Director: John Ford. Producer: Bernard Smith. Scenarist: James R. Webb, from Mari Sandoz's book. Photography (in color and Panavision): William Clothier. Art director: Richard Day. Music: Alex North. Editor: Otho Lovering. Filmed in Monument Valley; Moab, Utah; Gunnison, Colorado. With Richard Widmark, Carroll Baker, James Stewart, Edward G. Robinson, Karl Malden, Sal Mineo, Dolores Del Rio, Ricardo Montalban, Gilbert Roland, Arthur Kennedy, Patrick Wayne, Elizabeth Allen, John Carradine, Victor Jory, George O'Brien, Harry Carey, Jr., Ben Johnson, Willis Bouchey, Dan Borzage. 159 minutes.

Seven Women, 1966 (released in January) (Ford-Smith Productions–Metro-Goldwyn-Mayer). Director: John Ford. Producer: Bernard Smith. Scenarists: Janet Green, John McCormick, from Norah Lofts's story "Chinese Finale." Photography (in color and Panavision): Joseph La Shelle. Art directors: George W. Davis, Eddie Imazu. Music: Elmer Bernstein. Editor: Otho S. Lovering. With Anne Bancroft, Sue Lyon, Margaret Leighton, Flora Robson, Mildred Dunnock, Betty Field, Anna Lee, Eddie Albert, Mike Mazurki, Woody Strode. 87 minutes.

CHARLES IVES

I have listed these pieces (following the descriptions of John Kirk-patrick in *Charles E. Ives Memos* [New York: Norton, 1972], appendixes 3–4, pp. 152–77) by the titles I employed in my text. Song titles of *114 Songs* are not listed separately.

Adeste Fidelis, organ prelude, 1897 (Music Press 1949, later Mercury).

All the Way Around and Back, scherzo, piano (2 players), violin, clarinet, bells or French horn, bugle, before 1908 (Peer 1971).

America Variations, organ, 1891 (Music Press 1949; later Mercury).

Anti-Abolitionist Riots in 1830s and 40s, piano, 1908–9 (Mercury 1949).

Calcium Light Night (*The Gong on the Hook and Ladder, Firemen's Parade on Main Street*), strings, flute, clarinet, bassoon, 2 trumpets, trombone, piano, drums; triangle, bass drum, and cymbals *ad lib.*; before 1912 (Peer 1955).

Central Park in the Dark Some 40 Years Ago, for orchestra, 1906 (Peer 1968).

Chorales, see *Harvest Home Chorales*.

Concord Sonata (*Second Pianoforte Sonata*), 1909–15; I, *Emerson*; II, *Hawthorne*; III, *The Alcotts*; IV, *Thoreau* (privately printed, 1920; revised Arrow 1947; now Associated).

Decoration Day, see *Holidays*.

First Piano Sonata, 7 movements, 1902–9 (Peer 1954).

Fourth of July, see *Holidays*.

General William Booth's Entrance into Heaven, chorus or solo voice, originally brass band; later arranged for chamber orchestra by Becker, 1934 (*19 Songs*, by New Music 1935; now Merion).

Halloween, allegro vivace, string quartet and piano, 1906 (Peer 1961).

Harvest Home Chorales: Harvest Home, 1898 (text by Burgess); *Lord of the Harvest*, before 1902 (text by Gurney); *Harvest Home* before 1902 (text by Alford) (Mercury 1949).

Holiday Quick Step, brass band, 1887 (survives in manuscript fragments only, a set of parts in George Ives's hand, piccolo, 2 cornets in A, 2 violins, piano).

Holidays (Holidays Symphony): Washington's Birthday, for strings, flute, horn, and bells, 1909 (New Music 1936; now Associated); *Decoration Day*, for full orchestra, 1912 (ABC 1913); *Fourth of July*, for full symphony orchestra, 1912–13 (*New Music* and Edition Adler 1932; now Associated); *Thanksgiving*, for full orchestra and chorus, 1904 (Peer).

The Housatonic at Stockbridge, see *Three Places in New England*.

The Last Reader, English horn or clarinet, strings, 2 flutes, 1911 (Peer 1967).

Lincoln, the Great Commoner (text by Markham), 1912 (New Music 1932; now Merion).

Majority, The Masses, song, 1915, arranged 1921 (*19 Songs*, New Music 1935).

Orchestral Sets:

  First Orchestral Set, see *Three Places in New England*.

  Second Orchestral Set, for symphony orchestra, 1912–15: I, *An Elegy to Our Forefathers*; II, *The Rockstrewn Hills Join in the People's Outdoor Meeting*; III, *From Hanover Square North at the End of a Tragic Day, the People Again Arose* (Peer).

  Third Orchestral Set, 3 movements, 1919–26 (unfinished and unpublished).

Piano, see *First Piano Sonata, Concord Sonata, Sonatas for Violin and Piano*.

Psalm 67, for unaccompanied chorus, 1894 or 1898 (Arrow 1939; now Associated).

Putnam's Camp, see *Three Places in New England*.

Quartets:

  First Quartet, A Revival Meeting (or *Revival Service*), chorale, prelude, offertory, and postlude, 1896 (Peer 1961).

  Second String Quartet, 1911–13 (Peer 1954; revised 1970).

The Saint-Gaudens in Boston Common, see *Three Places in New England*.

Set for Theater or Chamber Orchestra: In the Cage, In the Inn, In the Night, 1906 (New Music 1932; now Merion).

Some Southpaw Pitching (Study No. 21), piano, 1908 (Mercury 1949).

Sonatas for Violin and Piano:

  First Sonata, 1903–8 (Peer 1953).

Second Sonata, 3 movements, 1903–9 [1902–9, 1907–10, 1904–
10, 1903–10] (Schirmer, 1951).

Third Sonata, 4 movements, 1905–14 (New Music 1951; now
Merion).

Fourth Sonata, 1906–9 [1906, 1909–10] (Arrow 1942; Associated).

see also *First Piano Sonata, Concord Sonata.*

Songs:

114 Songs, ?1887–1921 (privately printed 1921 [?1922] by Ives;
now Peer).

50 Songs (privately printed 1923 by Ives), shortened version of
above because of mix-up over Ives's free offer of copies of *114
Songs.*

7 Songs, 1902–21 (Cos Cob Press, 1932; later Arrow; now Associated).

34 Songs, 1889–1921 (New Music 1932; Merion).

18 [19] Songs, 1894–1925 (New Music 1935; Merion).

6 Songs, 1898–1920 (Mercury 1950).

4 Songs (Peer 1953).

12 Songs (Peer 1954).

14 Songs (Peer 1955).

9 Songs (Peer 1956).

13 Songs (Peer 1958).

[12] Sacred Songs (Peer 1961).

11 Songs and 2 Harmonizations (Associated 1968).

See *Charles E. Ives Memos*, by Kirkpatrick, appendix 4, for individual titles and which of these collections they appear in, and
for other information on revisions, etc.

Study No. 9, see *Anti-Abolitionist Riots in 1830s and 40s.*

Study No. 21, see *Some Southpaw Pitching.*

Study No. 22, see *Three-Page Sonata.*

Sunrise, song for voice, trio, and piano, 1926 (apparently Ives's last
composition).

Symphonies:

First Symphony, for large orchestra, 1896–98 (Peer 1971).

Second Symphony, 5 movements, for large orchestra (Southern
1951).

Third Symphony, 1904 (Arrow 1947; now Associated).

Fourth Symphony, 4 movements, for large orchestra, 1910–16 (1st and 2nd movements, New Music; Associated 1966).

see also *Holidays*, *Universe Symphony*.

Thanksgiving, see *Holidays*

Three-Page Sonata (Study No. 22), piano, 1905 (New Music 1947; Mercury 1949; revised Merion 1972).

Three Places in New England: I, *The Saint-Gaudens in Boston Common*, 1911; *Putnam's Camp*, 1912; *The Housatonic at Stockbridge*, before May 1911; (Birchard 1935; later Mercury).

Tone Roads, chamber orchestra: Fast, 1911; Slow, 1911–19; Slow and Fast, 1915 (No. 1, Peer 1949; No. 3, Peer 1952).

Trio, violin, cello, piano, 1904–11 (Peer 1955).

The Unanswered Question, A Cosmic Landscape, trumpet, 4 flutes, treble woodwind, and string orchestra, 1906–8 (*Pan American Bulletin of Music* 1941).

Universe Symphony, 1914–16 (ms.).

Washington's Birthday, see *Holidays*.

SELECTED BIBLIOGRAPHY

WILLIAM FAULKNER

Adams, Richard P. *Faulkner: Myth in Motion*. Princeton: Princeton University Press, 1968.

Bassett, John, ed. *Faulkner: The Critical Heritage*. London: Routledge & Kegan Paul Ltd., 1975.

Beck, Warren. *Faulkner: Essays*. Madison: University of Wisconsin Press, 1976.

Bedell, George C. *Kierkegaard and Faulkner: Modalities of Existence*. Baton Rouge: Louisiana State University Press, 1972.

Blotner, Joseph. *William Faulkner: A Biography*. New York: Random House, 1972.

Blotner, Joseph, ed. *Selected Letters of William Faulkner*. New York: Random House, 1977.

Brooks, Cleanth. *The Hidden God: Studies in Hemingway, Faulkner, Yeats, Eliot, and Warren*. New Haven: Yale University Press, 1963.

———. *The Yoknapatawpha Country*. New Haven: Yale University Press, 1963.

———.

Broughton, Panthea Reid. *William Faulkner: The Abstract and the Actual*. Baton Rouge: Louisiana State University Press, 1974.

Brylowski, Walter. *Faulkner's Olympian Laugh: Myth in the Snopes Novels*. Detroit, Mich.: Wayne State University Press, 1968.

Campbell, Harry Modean, and Foster, Ruel E. *William Faulkner: A Critical Appraisal*. New York: Cooper Square Publishers, (c. 1951) 1970.

Coindreau, Jaurice Edgar. *The Time of William Faulkner: A French View of Modern American Fiction*. Edited by George McMillan Reeves. Columbia: University of South Carolina Press, 1971.

Coughlan, Robert. *The Private World of William Faulkner*. New York: Harper, 1954.

Cullen, John B., and Watkins, Floyd C. *Old Times in the Faulkner Country*. Chapel Hill: University of North Carolina Press, 1961.

Cowley, Malcolm. *Faulkner-Cowley File: Letters and Memories, 1944–62*. New York: Viking, 1966.

Davis, Thadious M. *Faulkner's "Negro": Art and the Southern Context*. Baton Rouge: Louisiana State University Press, 1983.

Gold, Joseph. *William Faulkner: A Study in Humanism, from Metaphor to Discourse*. Norman: University of Oklahoma Press, 1966.

Hoffman, Frederick John. *William Faulkner*. New York: Twayne, 1961.

Hoffman, Frederick John, and Vickery, Olga W., eds. *William Faulkner: Three Decades of Criticism*. East Lansing: Michigan State University Press, 1960.

Holland, Norman N. *Five Readers Reading*. New Haven, Conn.: Yale University Press, 1975.

Howe, Irving. *William Faulkner: A Critical Study*. New York: Random House, 1952.

Hunt, John Wesley. *William Faulkner: Art in Theological Tension*. Syracuse: Syracuse University Press, 1965.

Irwin, John T. *Doubling and Incest (Repetition and Revenue): A Speculative Reading of Faulkner*. Baltimore: Johns Hopkins University Press, 1975.

Kawin, Bruce F. *Faulkner and Film*. New York: F. Ungar, 1977.

Kerr, Elizabeth Margaret. *William Faulkner's Gothic Domain*. Port Washington, N.Y.: Kennikat Press, 1979.

Kinney, Arthur F. *Faulkner's Narrative Poetics: Style as Vision*. Amherst: University of Massachusetts Press, 1978.

Kupferburg, John M. *Voice and Eye in Faulkner's Fiction*. Athens: University of Georgia Press, 1983.

Langford, Gerald. *Faulkner's Revision of "Absalom, Absalom": A Collation of the Manuscript and the Published Book*. Austin: University of Texas Press, 1971.

―――. *Faulkner's Revision of "Sanctuary": A Collation of the Unrevised Galleys and the Published Book*. Austin: University of Texas Press, 1972.

Malin, Irving. *William Faulkner: An Interpretation*. Stanford, Calif.: Stanford University Press, 1957.

Massey, Linton R. *"Man Working," 1919–1962: William Faulkner*. Catalogue of the William Faulkner Collection at the University of Virginia. Charlottesville: Bibliographical Society of the University of Virginia, 1968.

Matthews, John T. *The Play of Faulkner's Language*. Ithaca, N.Y.: Cornell University Press, 1982.

Meriwether, James B. *The Literary Career of William Faulkner*. Princeton: Princeton University Library, 1961.

Michel, Laurence Anthony. *The Thing Contained: Theory of the Tragic*. Bloomington: Indiana University Press, 1970.

Miner, Ward L. *The World of William Faulkner*. New York: Grove Press, 1952.

Minter, David L. *William Faulkner: His Life and Work*. Baltimore: Johns Hopkins University Press, 1980.

Pikoulis, John. *The Art of William Faulkner*. Totowa, N.J.: Barnes and Noble, 1982.

Pilkington, John. *The Heart of Yoknapatawpha*. Jackson: University Press of Mississippi, 1981.

Powers, Lyon Harris. *Faulkner's Yoknapatawpha Comedy*. Ann Arbor: University of Michigan Press, 1980.

Reed, Joseph W. *Faulkner's Narrative*. New Haven, Conn.: Yale University Press, 1974.

Richardson, Harold Edward, *William Faulkner: The Journey of Self-Discovery*. Columbia: University of Missouri Press, 1969.

Robb, Mary Cooper. *William Faulkner: An Estimate of His Contribution to the Modern American Novel*. Pittsburgh: University of Pittsburgh Press, 1957.

Skei, Hans H. *William Faulkner, the Short Story Career: an Outline of Faulkner's Short Story Writing from 1919 to 1962*. New York: Columbia University Press, 1981.

Slatoff, Walter Jacob. *Quest for Failure: A Study of William Faulkner*. Ithaca, N.Y.: Cornell University Press, 1960.

Smart, George K. *Religious Elements in Faulkner's Early Novels: A Selective Concordance*. Coral Gables, Fla.: University of Miami Press, 1965.

Stonum, Gary Lee. *Faulkner's Career: An Internal Literary History*. Ithaca, N.Y.: Cornell University Press, 1979.

Strandberg, Victor H. *A Faulkner Overview: Six Perspectives* (Port Washington, N.Y.: Kennikat Press, 1981.

Sundquist, Eric J. *Faulkner: The House Divided*. Baltimore: Johns Hopkins University Press, 1983.

Swiggart, Peter. *The Art of Faulkner's Novels*. Austin: University of Texas Press, 1962.

Taylor, Walter. *Faulkner's Search for a South*. Urbana: University of Illinois Press, 1983.

Thompson, Lawrance, *William Faulkner: An Introduction and Interpretation*. New York: Barnes & Noble, 1963.

Vickery, Olga W. *The Novels of William Faulkner: A Critical Interpretation*. Baton Rouge: Louisiana State University Press, 1959.

Waggoner, Hyatt. *William Faulkner*. Lexington: University Press of Kentucky, 1959.

Warren, Robert Penn. *Faulkner: A Collection of Critical Essays*. Englewood Cliffs, N.J.: Prentice-Hall, 1966.

Watson, James Gray. *The Snopes Dilemma: Faulkner's Trilogy*. Coral Gables, Fla.: University of Miami Press, 1968.

Wilde, Meta Carpenter, and Borsten, Orin. *A Loving Gentleman: The Love Story of William Faulkner and Meta Carpenter*. New York: Simon and Schuster, 1976.

Williams, David L. *Faulkner's Women: The Myth and the Muse*. Montreal: McGill–Queens University Press, 1977.

Wittenberg, Judith Bryant. *Faulkner: The Transfiguration of Biography*. Lincoln: University of Nebraska Press, 1979.

JOHN FORD

For this bibliography, as for so many other scholarly gifts I am indebted to Jeanine Basinger, a national treasure.

Anderson, Lindsay, *About John Ford* (London: Plexus, 1981).

Baxter, John, *The Cinema of John Ford* (London: A. Zwemmer, The International Film Guide Series, 1971).

Bogdanovich, Peter, *John Ford* (London: Cinema One, 1967; revised, Berkeley: University of California Press, 1978).

Ford, Dan, *Pappy*. New York.

McBride, Joseph, and Wilmington, Michael, *John Ford* (New York: Da Capo Press, 1975).

Nichols, Dudley, and Ford, John, *Stagecoach: a film of John Ford and Dudley Nichols* (New York: Simon and Schuster, 1971).

Place, Janey Ann, *The non-Western Films of John Ford* (Secaucus, N.J.: Citadel Press, 1979).

———. *The Western Films of John Ford* (Secaucus, N.J.: Citadel Press, 1974).

Sarris, Andrew, *The John Ford Movie Mystery* (Bloomington, Ind.: Indiana University Press, 1976).

Sinclair, Andrew, *John Ford* (New York: Dial Press, 1979).

The best dissertations on Ford are:

Budd, Michael Nathan, "A Critical Analysis of Western Films Directed by John Ford from STAGECOACH to CHEYENNE AUTUMN," University of Iowa, 1975.

Gallagher, Thomas Augustus, Jr., "The Movies of John Ford," Columbia University, 1978.

Lehman, Peter Robert, "John Ford and the Auteur Theory," University of Wisconsin, 1978.

Place, Janey Ann, "John Ford and a Semiology of Film," University of California at Los Angeles, 1975.

Articles through the end of 1975 (83 in number) are listed in Wilmington and McBride, *John Ford*, cited above. The most significant since then:

Badder, D. J. "John Ford," *Film Dope*, April 1979.

Beck, P., "Orson Welles and John Ford," *History and Myth in Film. UFAJ*, no. 3, 1976.

Browne, Nick, "The Spectator-in-the-Text: The Rhetoric of STAGECOACH," *Film Quarterly*, 29. no. 2, 1976.

Budd, M., "A Home in the Wilderness: Visual Imagery in John Ford," *Cinema Journal* 16, no. 1, 1976.

————. "Genre, Director, and Stars in John Ford's Westerns," *Wide Angle*, no. 4, 1978.

Byron, Stuart, "THE SEARCHERS: Cult Movie of the New Hollywood, *New York Magazine*, 12.45–48, Mar. 5, 1979.

Cadbury, W., "Semiology, Human Nature, and John Ford: the Contribution of Depth psychological and other theoretical resonances to Film Meaning," *Cinemonkey*, no. 19, 1979.

Combs, R., "John Ford: Shadow and Substance," *MFB*, June 1980.

Coursen, D., "John Ford Reprints the Legend," *Movietone News*, 42, July 1975.

————. "John Ford's Wilderness: THE MAN WHO SHOT LIBERTY VALANCE," *Sight and Sound*, no. 4, 1978.

Coursen, D., and Dempsey, M., "John Ford: Assessing the Reassessment," *Film Quarterly*, Spring 1976.

Ellis, K., "On the Warpath. John Ford and Indians," *Journal of Popular Film*, no. 2, 1980.

Everett, E. K., "The Hollywood People . . . and Other Things: John Ford, Movie Actor," *Classic Film Collector*, Spring 1978.

Goodwin, M., "Home Cinema: John Ford: A Poet Who Shot Great Movies," *Moving Image*, December 1981.

Greenfield, P., "Print the Fact: For and against John Ford," *Take One*, no. 12, 1977.

Jensen, N. "Fordiana," *Kosmorama* XXII/132, Winter 1976.

Lehman, P., "An Absence Which Becomes a Legendary Presence: John Ford's Structured Use of Off-Screen Space," *Wide Angle*, no. 4, 1978.

————. "Looking at Look's Missing Reverse Shot: Psychoanalysis and Style in John Ford's THE SEARCHERS," *Wide Angle*, no. 4, 1981.

McCarthy, Todd, "John Ford and Monument Valley," *American Film*, May 1978.

Mitry, Jean, "The Birth of a Style," *Wide Angle*, no. 4, 1978.

Place, Janey Ann, "A Family in a Ford," *Film Comment*, Sept.– Oct., 1976.

Pye, Douglas, "John Ford and the Critics, *Movie* 22, Spring 1976.

Roth, L., "Frontier Families: John Ford, Sergio Leone, Winning the West in American and Italian Style," *American Screen Classic*, no. 4, 1981.

Silver, Charles, "The Apprenticeship of John Ford," *American Film*, May 1976 (on the early films, 1917 to mid-Thirties).

Sinclair, Andrew, "John Ford's War," *Sight and Sound*, no. 2, 1979.

Siska, W. C., "Realism and Romance in the Films of John Ford," *Wide Angle*, no. 4, 1978.

Stowell, H. P., "John Ford's Literary Sources: from Realism to Romance," *Literature and Film Quarterly*, no. 2, 1977.

Taylor, B. "Ford and Peckinpah," *Framework*, Winter 1977.

CHARLES IVES

Charles Ives Centennial Festival: An Exhibition of Original Manuscripts and Song Recital, October 17, 1974, in the Museum and Library . . . National Institute of Arts and Letters. New York: National Institute, 1974.

Cowell, Henry, and Cowell, Sidney. *Charles Ives and His Music.* New York: Oxford University Press, 1955.

De Lerma, Dominique-Réné. *Charles Edward Ives 1874–1954: A Bibliography of His Music.* Kent, Ohio: Kent State University Press, 1970.

Elkus, Jonathan. *Charles Ives and the American Band Tradition: A Centennial Tribute*. Exeter: University of Exeter American Arts Documentation Centre, 1974.

Hitchcock, Hugh Wiley. *Ives*. London: Oxford University Press, 1977.

Ives, Charles Edward, *Essays Before a Sonata and Other Writings*. Edited by Howard Boatwright. New York: Norton, 1962.

————. *Memos*. Edited by John Kirkpatrick. New York: Norton, 1972.

Perlis, Vivian. *Charles Ives Remembered: An Oral History*. New Haven: Yale University Press, 1974.

Perry, Rosalie Sandra. *Charles Ives and the American Mind*. Kent, Ohio: Kent State University Press, 1974.

Rossiter, Frank R. *Charles Ives and His America*. New York: Liveright, 1975.

Warren, Richard. *Charles E. Ives: Discography*. New Haven, Conn.: Yale University Library Historical Sound Recordings, 1972.

Wooldridge, David. *From the Steeples and Mountains: A Study of Charles Ives*. New York: Knopf, 1974.

NOTES

PROLOGUE: IN THE AMERICAN GRAIN

1. G. K. Chesterton, *New York Times Magazine*, 28 June 1931.
2. Rudyard Kipling, *An American*.
3. Bernard Shaw, commenting on the award of the Nobel Prize to Sinclair Lewis, 1931.
4. Mark Twain, *My First Lie*.
5. Owen Wister, *The Virginian* [1902] (Boston: Houghton Mifflin Co., 1968), p. 23.
6. Ibid., p. 126.
7. Alexis de Tocqueville, *Democracy in America*, p. 244.
8. Michael Paul Rogin, *Subversive Genealogies*, New York, 1983, p. 109.
9. Ralph Waldo Emerson, *Society and Solitude: Success*.
10. Edmund Burke, *Conciliation with America*.
11. "The next Augustan Age will dawn on the other side of the Atlantic," Horace Walpole, letter to Sir Horace Mann, 24 Nov. 1774, *Correspondence* (New Haven: Yale University Press, 1967), xxiv. 62
12. Letter to his father, 1868 (aetat 24), Lloyd Goodrich, *Thomas Eakins* (Cambridge: Harvard University Press, 1982), i. 31.
13. Charles Ives, *Essays Before a Sonata and Other Writings*, p. 82.
14. Herman Melville, *Moby Dick* [493].
15. Raymund Fitzsimons, *Barnum in London*, 1970, pp. 4–5. See also Harriet Beecher Stowe, *Uncle Tom's Cabin* (chap. 23, 1979), p. 324, for an application of this pervasive metaphor (from the all-too-frequent steamboat explosions) to the slavery crisis:

    "They never shall get the upper hand!" said Alfred.
    "That's right," said St. Clare; "put on the steam, fasten down the escape-valve, and sit on it, and see where you'll land."
    "Well," said Alfred," we *will* see. I'm not afraid to sit on the escape-valve, as long as the boilers are strong, and the machinery works well."
    "The nobles in Louis XVI's time thought just so; and Austria and Pius IX think so now; and, some pleasant morning you may all be caught up to meet each other in the air, when the boilers burst."

16. *The Virginian*, p. 4.
17. Quoted in Rogin, p.
18. *Faulkner in the University*, p. 239.
19. In a collection on American film genre in preparation, a collaboration with Richard S. Slotkin and Joseph Reed. The term she suggests, which I trust will catch on (for this is more myth than narrative), is American Wawa: what we all have and have to make anew.
20. The student is Gao Wei, in his own way a telling student of our culture.
21. Ralph Waldo Emerson, *Uncollected Lectures: Character; Conduct of Life: Considerations by the Way; Uncollected Lectures, Books*.

22. Mark Twain, *A Connecticut Yankee in King Arthur's Court*, 1960 [1905–6], pp. 5, 16.
23. Ives, *Essays*, pp. 92–93.
24. Fitzsimons, *Barnum in London*, pp. 16–17.
25. Ralph Waldo Emerson, *Society and Solitude: Old Age*; Edmund Burke, *Conciliation with America*; Oscar Wilde, *A Woman of No Importance*; Oliver Wendell Holmes, *The Professor at the Breakfast Table*; Salvador de Madriaga, *Americans Are Boys*.
26. Ralph Waldo Emerson, *Thoughts on Art*, 1841.
27. Commissioners to municipal authorities of Bordeaux, 4 January 1793, quoted in *The Jeffersonian Creation*, ed. William Howard Adams, 1976, p. 235.
28. George Washington, letter to Samuel Vaughan, 5 Feb. 1785, *Writings*, 1931, 27.63.
29. *Lion in the Garden*, pp. 48, 61 [1940, 1948].
30. *Faulkner in the University*, p. 87 [1957].
31. *Lion in the Garden*, p. 222 [1955].
32. Charles Ives, *114 Songs*, (New York: Associated Music Publishers, Peer International Corp, Theodore Presser Co. [1975], Postface.
33. *Lion in the Garden*, p. 222 [1955].
34. Ives, *114 Songs*, Postface.
35. Emerson, *Conduct of Life: Considerations by the Way*.
36. Melville, *Moby Dick*, p. 143.
37. William Faulkner, "Addie," *As I Lay Dying*, 1957 [1930], p. 164.
38. Ibid., "Darl," p. 134.

ONE: ORIGINALS

1. My account is adapted from *William Faulkner: A Biography*, by Joseph Blotner, and other books listed in my bibliography.
2. This account is based on Lindsay Anderson, *About John Ford*; Andrew Sinclair, *John Ford*; Dan Ford, *Pappy*; and other titles listed in my bibliography.
3. Sinclair, *John Ford*, p. 9.
4. Francis Ford is most familiar for his later appearances in many bit parts in his brother's films (John begins as actor in the films Francis directs, Francis ends as actor in John Ford's movies), most memorably as the old soldier bidding farewell to the Shakespearean actor in *My Darling Clementine*.
5. Andrew Sinclair, Lindsay Anderson, Peter Bogdanovich et al.
6. Peter Bogdanovich, *John Ford*, 1967, p. 8.
7. Mary Astor, *A Life on Film*, p. 134, quoted in Anderson, *About John Ford*, p. 225.
8. Peter Bogdanovich, *John Ford*, 1967, p. 48. Selznick to Jock Whitney, 29 June 1937: "I . . . FEEL VERY STRONGLY, . . . THAT WE MUST SELECT THE STORY AND SELL IT TO JOHN FORD, INSTEAD OF HAVING FORD SELECT

SOME UNCOMMERCIAL PET OF HIS THAT WE WOULD BE MAKING ONLY BE-
CAUSE OF FORD'S ENTHUSIASM. I DO NOT THINK WE CAN MAKE ANY PIC-
TURE BECAUSE OF ANY DIRECTOR'S ENTHUSIASM, AND IF THIS MEANS WE
ARE TO LOSE FORD, I WILL SUPPLY [MERIAN C. COOPER] . . . WITH AS FINE
A DIRECTOR AS POSSIBLE. I SEE NO JUSTIFICATION FOR MAKING ANY STORY
JUST BECAUSE IT IS LIKED BY A MAN WHO, I AM WILLING TO CONCEDE, IS
ONE OF THE GREATEST DIRECTORS IN THE WORLD, BUT WHOSE RECORD
COMMERCIALLY IS FAR FROM GOOD." (*Memo from: David O. Selznick*,
1972, p. 155.) The picture Selznick didn't want to encourage Ford to
make was *The Stage to Lordsburg*—retitled *Stagecoach*.
9. Henry and Sidney Cowell, *Charles Ives and His Music*, p. v.
10. Charles Ives, *114 Songs*, Postface.

TWO: CANON

1. Vivian Perlis, *Charles Ives Remembered: An Oral History*, pp. 5–6.
2. Stanley Cavell, *The World Viewed*, 1971, pp. 55–59.
3. William Faulkner, *Light in August*, 1967, pp. 211–22; *Absalom, Absalom!*, 1951, pp. 222–25.
4. The Indian is another stray affinity; they have an oddly common atti-
tude toward the native American, a consciousness of what he meant
rather than just that he is a common subject category: Ives's song *The
Indians*, Faulkner's Indian stories of *Requiem for a Nun* and elsewhere,
and Ford's Indians throughout the Westerns would be the subject for a
dissertation. But their treatment of them is for their time without prejudice and never neglects their independent culture. Sentimental nostalgia or perhaps even some shade of emotional and unrepresentative
individualism sometimes characterizes it. Ives's song hails vanished an-
cestors, the now reduced culture. He does not so much mock as embody
their decay in the tom-tom parody tune he hauls out of the trunk to
undercut a very modern and very trickily breathless vocal line. And the
meeting of these two elements in their common space does more than
suggest two cultures. Faulkner could be accused of turning the native
American to comedy and perhaps (as he more frequently is accused of
doing to blacks) of never really getting inside the Indian's skin, but he
could not be charged with lack of sympathy or failure to espouse the
Indian's cause. Even debauched and debased in their corruption by
other cultures Faulkner's Indians still stalk the fictional country with
more dignity than either his whites or his blacks. If anything, Faulkner
should be charged with buying into an out-of-date mythic structure, for
there is perhaps more of the eighteenth century's Noble Savage in his
Indians than there is of Mississippi's remnant braves. Anyone willing
to make a joke of Ford's treatment of Indians in *Stagecoach* will want
to watch *Cheyenne Autumn* before speaking. To quote Faulkner, "They
endured."
5. The choice is not without political overtones. That representative of

regionalism which sees the outsider as enemy must be sure he can find an audience willing to lend majority to his cause and this is an apparent anomaly. But if this were all that difficult there would have been fewer American politicians who have succeeded in constructing winning national majorities with regional appeals. "Running against the mess in Washington" is a regional appeal finding a more general audience: something compels us to love being underdogs and then to overwhelm the opposition—to assemble with other underdogs until there are more of us than of them. Complex clichés such as this are more like Ford's, Faulkner's and Ives's Americanism—indeed, more like our own—than are jingoism or simplistic patriotism. The American was never a jingoist unless he also added something under his breath about underdogs.

6. See Chapter Four: Genre.
7. Ives is pointing out in the holidays which form his program for this piece: that Thanksgiving and the Fourth of July can be at one and the same time ritual enactments and instant nostalgia trips, that holidays by their nature inhabit both an any-time and an all-time, and that we, in turn, inhabit them in that double way.
7a. Kit Reed, *Story First*, 1982, p. 2.
8. Spig Wead (John Wayne), after crashing à training plane in the admiral's pool, goes on in a life of derring-do as a racing and stunt pilot publicizing Navy Air Arm, and seems to prefer this life and officers'-club shenanigans to life with his family, seen by him as somewhat alien. One of his children dies. Then in a freak accident on the stairs at home he breaks his back and, rejecting reunion with his wife Minnie (Maureen O'Hara), recovers slowly with the aid of Chief Carson (Dan Dailey) and the encouragement of the Chief's ukulele. He becomes a screenwriter for director John Dodge (Ward Bond). In World War II he pioneers experiments in the use of jeep carriers and after another possible but failed reunion with his wife suffers a heart attack at sea.
9. William Faulkner, *Light in August*, p. 467.
10. There was a momentary flap when a newspaper to which Ives had sent a copy of *114 Songs* quoted from it his offer of free copies to any who requested them (Charles Ives, "Letter to the Sun," *Essays*, pp. 132–33).
11. Joseph W. Reed, *Faulkner's Narrative*, p. 259; I return to this question at the end of the book. The photos by Henri Cartier-Bresson were done for Magnum Pictures: some illustrate *Faulkner at West Point*, 1964.
12. I am reminded of a canonical statement by Stanley Cavell on a very different matter: "My claim is that in the case of films, it is generally true that you do not really like the highest instances unless you also like typical ones. You don't even know what the highest are instances of unless you know the typical as well." (*The World Viewed*, enlarged, 1979, p. 6)
13. Terangi (Jon Hall), trusted mate on a sailing vessel in trade between his native island and Tahiti, strikes an Anglo in a bar, and is imprisoned.

He attempts many escapes (the first in a dive off a cliff and an unsuccessful swim to the departing schooner). Each time he adds months,
then years, to his sentence. Back on the island, DeLaage (Raymond
Massey) the by-the-book Governor of the island, refuses to intercede in
spite of the pleas of his wife (Mary Astor) and his friend the doctor
(Thomas Mitchell). Terangi's jailer (John Carradine) takes a more and
more personal and sadistic interest in his escape attempts. In an apparent attempt to hang himself, Terangi escapes, steals a boat and food in
the village, and undertakes alone the long trip through storms. He is
found adrift by the priest of his island (C. Aubrey Smith). At news of
the escape there is rejoicing, but it is followed by the rising wind of the
Great Storm. Terangi returns to the island during the hurricane with
his wife (Dorothy Lamour) and child, and saves the life of Madame
DeLaage. DeLaage comes upon him escaping by boat but refuses to
make chase. The doctor delivers a child in an open boat. The Island—
church, village, governor's bungalow—has been completely destroyed.
14. Guthrie McCabe (James Stewart), a corrupt sheriff set up in business
(and later hustled out of it) by a fancy lady, is engaged on behalf of a
wagon train by Lieutenant Jim Gary (Richard Widmark) to seek to ran-
som children captured years ago by Indians. McCabe is cynical, paints a
black picture for his employers while he's drunk, but goes through with
it, rides to Quanah Parker's camp, finds some whites and some sus-
pected whites, and he and Gary bring back a young man and a woman.
McCabe quarrels with Gary, splitting him off, to return the man to
camp and with himself takes Elena de la Madriaga (Linda Cristal), a
Mexican who has in captivity become Stone Calf's (Woody Strode's)
woman. McCabe kills Stone Calf unexpectedly; Elena mourns like a
squaw. On return to camp the young man is refused by his ransomers,
caged, released by his would-be mother (whom he kills) during the post
dance at which Elena is being snubbed by the ladies of the post. On his
way to his death by lynching, the youth upsets a music box, and his
recognition of its tune convinces Marty (Shirley Jones) that he is indeed her brother. McCabe returns to his town, finds his place has been
taken in the fancy lady's bed, in his chair, his clothes, his beer, and his
office (presumably also in his share of the take) by a gangly fool, and he
seeks California with Elena.
15. Sinclair, McBride, *passim.*
16. *La Règle du Jeu*, N.E.F. Productions, 1939; screenplay, dialogue, direction by Renoir (screenplay with the collaboration of Carl Koch); photographed by Jean Bachelet; with Marcel Dalio, Nora Gregor, Roland
Toutain, Jean Renoir (as Octave), Paulette Dubost, Gaston Modot.
17. I have always thought this model came from Charles Feidelson but he
recently pleaded innocence. Maybe it was in the air.

THREE: COMMUNITY

1. We have been hearing a church bell and have seen people going down a street toward what we think must be a church. Wyatt Earp meets Clementine in the hotel lobby; she takes his arm and they walk down the middle of a long porch, are greeted at its end by the town barber, turn to their left, and move, now behind the hotel, toward the sound of a congregation singing *Shall We Gather at the River?* We then see that the church is only a floor and a frame with flags. As they arrive the deacon ends the prayer and starts a dance. Wyatt thinks about it, asks her to dance and as they are dancing two of his brothers return in a buckboard from visiting the grave of the brother killed at the beginning of the movie, to see Wyatt, unaccustomedly dancing. (For a synopsis of the whole film, see n. 23 to this chapter.)
2. Joseph W. Reed, *Faulkner's Narrative*, pp. 278–79.
3. William Faulkner, *Sanctuary*, 108–9.
4. Ibid., pp. 288–89.
5. Ibid., pp. 308–09.
6. William Faulkner, *Light in August*, p. 272.
7. Ibid., p. 273.
8. William Faulkner, *The Hamlet*, p. 324; see also pp. 314–16.
9. William Faulkner, "Gavin Stevens," *The Town*, p. 278.
10. William Faulkner, *The Mansion*, 1959, p. 248.
11. Reed, *Faulkner's Narrative*, pp. 218–57.
12. *Boswell: Laird of Auchinleck, 1778–1782*, ed. Reed & Pottle, 1977, p. xxiii.
13. A stagecoach is headed to Lordsburg. Aboard are a bank employee making away with the bank's funds (Berton Churchill), a tart with a heart of gold (Claire Trevor), a Caspar Milquetoast (Donald Meek), a drunk doctor (Thomas Mitchell), a Southern aristocrat (John Carradine) and a pregnant woman (Louise Platt). On the way they are hailed by, and the stage picks up the Ringo Kid (John Wayne). Andy Devine drives. The child is born, Ringo and the tart fall in love, the doctor faces himself, and the stage is pursued by Indians, then saved by the cavalry just outside Lordsburg. There the Kid has a gunfight with the Plummer Brothers (who in prehistory victimized his family), and he and Dallas are sent off to his ranch (instead of a jail sentence) by the sheriff and the doctor.
14. China, 1935. A missionary compound is threatened by a bandit horde. Inside the compound are the head of station (Margaret Leighton); Emma Clark (Sue Lyon), hardly more than a girl; a pregnant woman (Betty Field) and her husband (Eddie Albert). Three more women arrive seeking safety, as does Doctor D. R. Cartwright (Anne Bancroft), the physician newly assigned there. Once captured, Cartwright sacrifices herself in exchange for the release of the other women.

15. We never see the outdoors to speak of, except for the bit of mounted horsemen in a rather unclear attack which runs under the movie's titles.
16. April 1863. A cavalry unit under Colonel John Marlowe (John Wayne) is sent by Grant on a raid, deep behind enemy lines, to destroy the railroad line at Newton Station. He unwillingly takes along Dr. Kendall (William Holden), and on a stop at a plantation, catches Hannah Hunter (Constance Towers) spying on them, so she and her black maid must come along. A rebel officer at the station leads a hopeless charge out of freight cars of an arriving train. On their return they are attacked by the boys of the Jefferson Military Academy. Marlowe, wounded, blows a bridge and leaves behind the doctor and Hannah Hunter to the Confederates to nurse the sick.
17. For synopsis, see above, chapter two, n. 8.
18. Lieutenant Colonel Kirby Yorke (John Wayne) takes over a command in the Western cavalry and discovers there his son Jeff (Claude Jarman, Jr.) in the ranks. His wife, Kathleen (Maureen O'Hara), who has been separated from him since Yorke had to burn her plantation during the war, comes to visit intending to buy Jeff out of the service. Kirby courts Kathleen. In an Indian raid, women and children en route to a safer fort are attacked and held prisoner in a church. The Cavalry rides, Kirby is wounded, Jeff removes the arrow, Kathleen takes his hand as he is dragged on a litter back into the station.
19. 1949, Warner Brothers, directed by Raoul Walsh. The story of a psychopath Cody Jarrett (James Cagney), his Ma (Margaret Wycherley), and his criminal struggle to the top of the world, which turns out to be a tank of high-octane fuel which, as Fallon (Edmond O'Brien) observes, blows up in his face. The movie is constructed in three stages: the first beginning in a train heist and moving through pursuit to Jarrett's surrender on a bum rap; the second in prison, leading to escape (but after Fallon has been introduced into Cody's friendship); and a final heist at an oil refinery involving a Trojan-Horse tanker truck, a radio homing-device cobbled up from Verna's (Virginia Mayo's) radio.
20. A PT-boat squadron, just about to get a chance to find a place in the peacetime navy, is caught in the losing withdrawal action in the Philippines. Lieutenant John Brickley (Robert Montgomery) and his exec., Lieutenant Rusty Ryan (John Wayne), fight capital ships, carry messages, see General Douglas MacArthur to safety, get separated, lose Rusty's girl, Lieutenant Sandy Davis (Donna Reed), on Bataan, lose much of their unit and finally their boats—Ryan's damaged and then destroyed, Brickley's dragged off through the jungle to do mail duty for the army. Leaving Chief Boots Mulcahey (Ward Bond) behind in command, Brickley and Ryan are ordered to fly to Australia in one of the last planes out.
21. Compare Wayne's speech (delivered through the reflection of the gallant line of blue) on the survival of the force in *Fort Apache*, and then realize the powerful chord Ford strikes as surely as did MacArthur in the

less-remembered of his Farewells, that to the Point: "Of the Corps, the Corps, the Corps."

22. Upper New York State, prior to the Revolution. Gil Martin (Henry Fonda) and Lana (Claudette Colbert) carve out a place and a farm as the English stir up trouble with the Indians. The farm is burned to the ground in an Indian attack and Lana has a miscarriage; the Widow McKlennan (Edna May Oliver) takes them in as tenants on her farm. Gil marches off with the settlement's detachment and returns wounded. Lana has a baby. The Indians attack the stockade, and when things look bad, Gil runs for help (outrunning three very fast Mohawks) and Lana in uniform takes her place on the firing line. Help arrives, the stockade is saved, the American flag is raised, and everyone goes back to work.

23. Wyatt Earp (Henry Fonda) and his brothers (Ward Bond, Tim Holt, Don Garner) are driving cattle near Tombstone. James is left behind to guard the herd; Wyatt quells a drunken Indian, is offered the marshalship, and refuses. He accepts when he returns finds James dead and the herd stolen. He duly meets Doc Holliday (Victor Mature) and his girl Chihuahua (Linda Darnell): Doc is the power in the town, and Clementine Carter (Cathy Downs), an Eastern nurse who knew Doc when he was respectable, comes to find him. Wyatt accompanies her one Sunday morning to the church building and the dance the folks celebrate its completion with. Old Man Clanton (Walter Brennan) and his boys kill Virgil Earp when he comes to get them for James's killing and Chihuahua dies in an operation on the pool table. The Clantons wait at the O.K. Corral for Wyatt, Doc, and Morgan Earp. Summarizing this film this way makes me more conscious even than did the other summaries of how inadequate a verbal account of the actions of a film are to what happens in that movie when we are present to it and it to us.

24. Travis Blue (Ben Johnson) and Sandy Owens (Harry Carey, Jr.), cowboys who are no better than they should be, sign on to see a group of Mormons on the way west. They meet up with a medicine show including Denver (Joanne Dru), which joins the train and Uncle Shiloh Clegg and his boys (Charles Kemper, Fred Libby, James Arness, Hank Worden, Mickey Simpson), who threateningly join it as well. Travis proposes to Denver and she refuses. When the Cleggs threaten the Mormons' wagons, Travis and Sandy in some fancy gunplay kill off the Cleggs.

25. 1948, Monterey Productions, directed by Howard Hawks, with John Wayne, Montgomery Clift, Joanne Dru, Harry Carey, Harry Carey, Jr., Walter Brennan.

26. See n. 14 to Chapter Two for synopsis.

27. Lieutenant Colonel Thursday (Henry Fonda), a commander by the book, takes command of this Western outpost, bringing Philadelphia (Shirley Temple) his daughter as hostess. She is attracted to Lieutenant Michael O'Rourke (John Agar), son of the sergeant major and his wife (Ward Bond and Irene Rich). Captain York (John Wayne) has been ne-

gotiating peace with Cochise of the Comanches. In the middle of the noncommissioned officers' ball, Thursday commands the post into battle against the Comanches in a doomed cavalry charge, by the book. They are decimated. Years later, York, now in command, recalls Thursday for a group of reporters.

FOUR: GENRE

1. When the waves softly sigh,
   When the sunbeams die;
   When the night shadows fall,
   Evening bells call,
   Margarita! Margarita! I think of thee!
   While the silver moon is gleaming,
   Of thee, I'm dreaming.

   Yale, Farewell! we must part,
   But in mind and heart,
   We shall ever hold thee near
   Be life gay or drear.
   Alma Mater! Alma Mater! we will think of thee!
   May the strength thou gavest
   Ever be shown in ways, fair to see.

   O have mercy Lord, on me,
   Thou art ever kind,
   O, let me oppressd with guilt,
   Thy mercy find.
   The joy thy favor gives, Let me regain
   Thy free spirit's firm support my fainting soul sustain.
   Lyrics for *A Song—for Anything* (No. 89 of *114 Songs* by Charles Ives). Copyright © 1955 by Peer International Corporation. Copyright renewed by Peer International Corporation. Copyright secured.
2. Charles Ives, *114 Songs*, Postface.
3. Ibid.
4. Ibid.
5. See Tom Wolfe, *From Our House to Bauhaus*.
6. Ives, *114 Songs*, Postface.
7. Ibid.
8. Ibid.
9. Ibid.
10. Ibid. Compare Faulkner's prefatory note to *The Mansion* and Ford's many offhand and practical responses to questions in various interviews.
11. A much better picture than it is given credit for. See, for instance, Selznick's contempt in *Memo from: David O. Selznick*, p. 155: "I SAW 'WEE WILLIE WINKIE' THE OTHER NIGHT AND IT IS ANYTHING BUT A GREAT PICTURE, AND IF YOU WILL ANALYZE FORD'S RECORD YOU WILL FIND THAT

BALANCED AGAINST ONE REALLY GREAT PICTURE, 'THE INFORMER' WHICH
CERTAINLY COULD NOT BE TERMED A COMMERCIAL SMASH, AND A COUPLE
OF GOOD PICTURES THAT DID FAIRLY WELL, SUCH AS 'THE LOST PATROL'
AND 'THE WHOLE TOWN'S TALKING,' ARE SUCH OUTSTANDING FAILURES
AS 'MARY OF SCOTLAND' AND 'THE PLOUGH AND THE STARS.' I THEREFORE
FEEL THAT WE MUST DISMISS FORD AS A MAN WHO IS NO MORE SURE-FIRE
THAN IS CUKOR. BOTH ARE GREAT DIRECTORS AND BOTH HAVE TO HAVE
THEIR STORIES SELECTED FOR THEM AND GUIDED FOR THEM, AND PRE-
SUMABLY FORD NEEDS THE SAME GUIDANCE IN SCRIPT THAT CUKOR
DOES."

12. After we are told there is a military school nearby filled with little boys, we see the school, the headmaster's office, and then see the troop parading forth with its headmaster in the lead, leaving two boys with mumps on the balcony. A mother asks the headmaster to let her have one boy, her last, and the headmaster grants it, although the boy so resists his mother that he follows his thrown drum out an upstairs window and rejoins the troop in its charge on John Wayne's cavalry raiding party. Wayne retreats so as not to kill the boys who are beginning to pick off his troops.

13. In Basinger-Reed-Slotkin, *Imaginary Rules*, in process.

14. I think it likely that De Mille went to his grave thinking Griffith was his competition. In a sense, of course—that sense in which every director must deal with the anxiety of influence about his greatest predecessor—Griffith indeed was. But De Mille seems to have thought so into the Fifties.

EPILOGUE: AGAINST THE GRAIN

1. Richard Slotkin, *Regeneration Through Violence* (Middletown, Conn.: Wesleyan University Press, 1973), and its sequels in process.

2. Charles Ives, *Essays-American Myth*, pp. 139ff., 200 ff., 215 ff.

3. William Faulkner, *Essays, Speeches, and Public Letters*, ed. James F. Meriwether (New York: Random House, p. 224).

4. Andrew Sinclair, *John Ford*, pp. 210–11, Joe McBride and Michael Wilmington, *John Ford*, pp. 13–14.

5. Chapter Two, n. 4.

6. Lindsay Anderson, "The Quiet Man," in *Sequence* (New Year, 1952), p. 26.

7. Lindsay Anderson, "John Ford," *Cinema* 6, no. 2 (Spring 1971).

8. For this, as for so many ideas in these essays, I am indebted to Jon K. Barlow.

9. Andrew Sinclair in his biography (and other critics) pursue this argument of Catholicism, often lumping *The Fugitive* with *Three Godfathers*. I think not.

10. *My Darling Clementine, They Were Expendable, The Mansion*.

11. This corresponds, all too closely, to various attitudes toward Ford as artist, Ford as popular movie maker. See the Selznick fallacy, n. 11 above.

12. "This book was written three years ago. To me it is a cheap idea, because it was deliberately conceived to make money. I had been writing books for about five years, which got published and not bought. But that was all right. . . . I could do a lot of things that could earn what little money I needed, thanks to my father's unfailing kindness which supplied me with bread at need, despite the outrage to his principles at having been of a bum progenitive. . . . I began to think about making money by writing. . . . I took a little time out, and speculated what a person in Mississippi would believe to be the current trends, chose what I thought was the right answer and invented the most horrific tale I could imagine and sent it to Smith, who had done *The Sound and the Fury* and who wrote me immediately, 'Good God, I can't publish this, We'd both be in jail.' . . . and I made a fair job and I hope you will buy it and tell your friends and I hope they will buy it too. . . . New York, 1932." (*Sanctuary*, Modern Library ed., pp. v–viii)

13. Paul Rotha, *The Film Till Now*, 1935, pp. 50, 130, 132, 133.

14. See Stuart Byron, "THE SEARCHERS: Cult Movie of the New Hollywood," *New York Magazine*, 12. 45–48, 5 March 1979.

INDEX

All proper names and selected subjects have been indexed, including the filmography for Ford; the bibliography and listings of principal works of Faulkner and Ives have not been included in the index, although entries for most of these will be found for appearances elsewhere in the book.

ABOUT THE AUTHOR

JOSEPH W. REED is a noted scholar of American Studies who has edited books and anthologies and written extensively on American history, literature, and film, including such diverse works as *Faulkner's Narrative*, two books of Horace Walpole, *Working with Kazan*, and *English Biography in the Early Nineteenth Century, 1801–1838*. He is also a painter, engraver, and graphic artist. Since 1971, he has been a professor of English, American Studies, and film at Wesleyan University. He is married to Kit Reed the novelist. His home is in Middletown, Connecticut.

ABOUT THE BOOK

THREE AMERICAN ORIGINALS was composed in Goudy Old Style by G & S Typesetters of Austin, Texas. The design is by Joyce Kachergis Book Design and Production of Bynum, North Carolina. The text stock is Warren's Olde Style, printed and bound at Vail-Ballou Press, Binghamton, New York. Wesleyan University Press, 1984.